Verification in economics and history

A sequel to 'scientifization'

O.F. Hamouda and B.B. Price

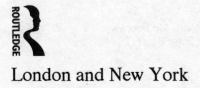

London and New York

First published 1991
by Routledge
11 New Fetter Lane, London EC4P 4EE

Simultaneously published in the USA and Canada
by Routledge
a division of Routledge, Chapman and Hall, Inc.
29 West 35th Street, New York, NY 10001

© 1991 O.F. Hamouda and B.B. Price

Typeset by NWL Editorial Services, Langport, Somerset

Printed and bound in Great Britain by Biddles Ltd,
Guildford and King's Lynn

British Library Cataloguing in Publication Data
Hamouda, O.F. (Omar F.)
    Verification in economics and history: a sequel to
    scientifization
    1. Economics. Methodology 2. Historiology. Methodology
    I. Title II. Price, B.B. (Betsy Barker) *1951–*
    330.01

    ISBN 0–415–05336–6

Library of Congress Cataloging in Publication Data
Hamouda, O.F.
Verification in economics and history: a sequel to
scientifization/O.F. Hamouda and B.B. Price
Includes bibliographical references.
Includes index.
ISBN 0–415–05336–6
1. Economics – Methodology 2. History – Methodology.
3. Verfication (Logic) I. Price, B.B. (Betsy Barker), 1948–
II. Title
HB71.H385 1991   90–474233
330'072–dc20   CIP

Contents

Preface

Economics and history are both disciplines devoted to the study of phenomena or events in which human action is the determinant. Each considers the individual both alone and in the context of societal interactions and intricate relations with the material world. Although their timeframes might be different (as economics clearly tries to embrace the future), these disciplines might be thought to share some characteristics of the methodology of their investigation and the ontology of their subject matter. The events affecting individuals in a social dynamic context pose specific ontological peculiarities: these events may occur once and for all or repeatedly; they may affect an individual or the aggregate. If the aim of a discipline which studies them is to attempt to explain them, then distinctive methodological concerns also surface.

To understand the ontological peculiarities and distinctive methodological concerns of economics and history, one might begin by asking what the characteristics of the phenomena and events under their study are. How do economists and historians construct plausible theories which both describe and explain the characteristics of phenomena and events which constantly change, never repeat, and cannot be isolated for observation? There is a widespread practice in economics, adhered to by some in history as well, of resorting to quantitative methods, which use both mathematical and statistical symbols and procedures, to build models and to provide criteria for the acceptance or rejection of theories. This method is believed, by many, to be the scientific approach, able to yield value-free, sound explanations. Rather than being questioned, the use of such practices seems to be increasing, especially with the continued development of the computer to data collect and number crunch at an ever faster rate.

Limitations in the quantitative method present themselves

precisely because of the nature of the phenomena of economic and historical interest, as well as the actual state of development in mathematics and probability, and the yield of statistical data compared to the varieties of other evidence available. It is argued in this book that the use of quantitative methods in model building and in an ensuing data-based verification step is neither sufficient nor always necessary to validate or invalidate knowledge. A quantitative methodology does not constitute in and of itself a scientific approach; often what is considered empirical evidence is theory-laden. Further, verifying a theory against selected data becomes a circular process; one quantified abstraction is simply verified by another abstraction. The empirical nature of the investigation is lost.

Indeed, there is one universal problem economists and historians, like all other scholars, must confront in their efforts to provide an explanation of the phenomena under study, and it is the very one which has made quantitative methods so attractive to scientists and non-scientists alike. A correspondence between the theoretical expression of the characteristics of the phenomena and the actual manifestation of those phenomena has to be established. Given that an exact match of theoretical component and phenomenological element is difficult, or rather impossible, to establish, the method-ological step of verification plays an important role in ensuring that a particular correspondence has meaning. The present study is about what the roles and the purpose of verification are and could be in establishing knowledge. It presents the conceptual difficulties these entail.

A discussion of the roles and purpose of verification will focus in this study on the theory–phenomena correspondence in the disci-plines of Economics and History and address thereby related epistemological, as well as ontological and methodological issues. The meaning of verification is understood here to include the notions of confirmation, falsification, and modification. It is argued that the role of verification, checking the theory against data as popularized in the practice of quantitative methods in economics and history, is too constraining, and needs to be reconsidered; that one role should come to play but a small part in the verifying process. Its whole scope should be much broader and its function much more important. Verifying could come to mean the process of weighing a theory's potential and of finding 'sense' in its arguments.

The topic of verification is deemed an important one. Since the members of the Vienna Circle in the 1920s transformed the classical empiricism of Bacon, Hume and Mill into logical positivism, much has been written on the concepts of verifiability, falsifiability, and confirmability in the sciences. It is ironic that when scientists and the philosophers of science are challenging the meaning of 'scientific law' and raising questions as to the status of 'truth' in science, social scientists are still vigorously reinforcing the idea of scientific and universal truth. Whole schools of thought in the humanities and social sciences have followed and still continue to follow in the steps of Neo-positivist philosophy of science, trying hard to 'raise' their disciplines to the status of science. Social scientists have borrowed their name, and some have even adopted methods of science, such as conceiving theories on universal principles and hypotheses and attempting to validate findings through empirical verification. The debate concerning the implications of neo-positivism, considered *passé* in philosophy of science, is only just beginning in the social sciences and its discussions are yet to be developed.

John Hicks, a leading twentieth-century economist and one of the founders of both mathematical economics and the modern dynamic approach to the study, captured, in a single statement, the essence of economics: 'As economics pushes on beyond "statics" it becomes less like science, and more like history' (Hicks 1979: xi). After five decades of contributions to model building and pure economic theory, Hicks had come to realize that abstract economic constructs, including the most recent mathematical dynamic developments, are, at most, descriptive theories of *how* things are related. Mathematics and statistics, he realized, cannot be made to carry the burden of causal explanation. None the less, by extending their formal theories, economists more and more frequently interpret the calculus of their models to infer causal relations from correlations and to advance explanations for *why* things have occurred. Aided by their formal theories, economists, like historians, attempt thus to explain actual economic phenomena, providing explanation from the assembled pieces of extant information. It is not uncommon, however, in economics, to find the process of the exercise reversed, that information is sought to support already conceived elaborate theories, a practice useful perhaps as an intellectual exercise for developing the imaginable, but probably less useful as an explanation of phenomena.

It is believed by many economists and some historians that the phenomena they study are (or behave *as if* they are) regulated by laws of nature. This belief has led many to use the same tools as physics – a strict methodology, quantification and mathematization whenever possible. A companion and far more profound influence from the sciences has, however, also been effected on their concept of the role of causality in understanding the phenomena under study. The sciences since Galileo adopted a posture of abandoning the investigation of causes of material phenomena; the legacy from Aristotle had become frustrating and relatively fruitless, while the description of the phenomena had become technically more interesting and possible. With increasing conviction in their operationally deterministic nature, an emphasis on experimental laws for observed phenomena ensued; the deterministic nature meant that the discovery of experimental laws would suffice to render nature malleable and predictable, even without an explanatory understanding of the causes of its phenomena. In the context where phenomena studied are not of deterministic nature the understanding of causal relations becomes essential if an explanation of the dynamics of the phenomena is to be provided.

It is argued that the scientification of economics and history, which began independently and well before the development of neo-positivism, is in itself a good thing, since it encourages rigour both in methods of investigating as well as in the theoretical articulation of concepts and ideas. Recourse to empirical investigation is also necessary, since economics and history are about the observed world. The problem, however, lies in the misconception of the meaning of 'scientific' and what theories and observation can and cannot do. The belief that the study of social phenomena in economics and history is not any different from that of natural phenomena in the exact sciences has led to misconceptions in both disciplines. Despite their detection of apparent patterns in social dynamic processes, both groups act mistakenly if they consider the 'laws'[1] they derive from regularities to be laws of nature. Neither can their formulated abstract statements, however useful, serve a function analogous to statements in the pure sciences; nor can these disciplines' theories which derive from a mixture of hypothetical and factual statements also have the same purpose as scientific theory. In particular, the methods of verification in the social sciences, seen as empirical investigations, which consist mainly in validating behavioural hypotheses by subjecting them to pseudo-tests, are at the root of this misconception. They have instilled a confidence in the conclusions of observation and extended that confidence to a willingness, in the case of economists, to predict, and in the case of historians, to project.

Economists and historians are divided into many schools of thought. The present discussion is directed to the large dominating body of economists,[2] who emphasize both the use of quantitative methods in the making of theories and who rely on verification as the criterion for acceptance or rejection of these theories, and to the group of historians, especially the cliometricians, which has been influenced by economists. It is not intended to be a parallel study of the two disciplines. A great deal of history is averse to such methods and is only peripherally concerned with some aspects of the issues raised here. In fact, the methodological controversies of what constitutes explanation, that have been carried on among historians, will help to illustrate an issue which a large number of economists have taken as granted.

The concept of verification under discussion in the present book is a controversial issue, not only in economics and history, but to different degrees in almost all other disciplines, including, especially, philosophy. A concept of verification is itself related to other equally controversial philosophical concepts and cannot therefore easily be treated in isolation. The present study can be seen as deficient in many aspects. First, literature relevant to a reconsideration of the concept of verification is enormous, and only a tiny part of it could be addressed. Apologies are expressed to any authors whose work did not receive due consideration. (In defence of the charge of omission it might be said that the book is not intended to be a survey of the controversial literature on neo-positivism nor of the methodologies of either economics or history.[3]) Second, each discipline, if not each division within a discipline, seems to develop its own definitions of shared vocabulary. Great difficulty is encountered in sorting through the meanings attached to the same words by various scholars. At the risk of creating more confusion, effort was made in this text to fix once again a specific meaning to the most essential terms. Third, the notion of probability, which appeals in quantitative methods for the taking into account of the random nature of phenomena under study, is not discussed here; it is believed that its exclusion does not affect the main arguments. The use of probabilities in economics and history raises just as many questions as the concept of verification and requires a whole study in and of itself. Finally, the book is written by an economist and a historian. Their ideas may be seen by their own colleagues as foreign, and thus irrelevant, while scholars in other disciplines may find bits and pieces of the arguments derive from their domains, where they have already been explored at length. Both reactions will be deserved in part, but the aim of the book is to provide a multidisciplinary analysis from the perspective of economics and history.

In sum, the book is meant to be a reflection on the state of theories in economics and in history in the light of the process of verification and on the sequel to the disciplines' scientifization. With the tools of mathematics and physics demystified and mastered in quantitative methods in economics and even in history, it is deemed important to ask what the post-scientifization step will be.

We are grateful to Tony Lawson for encouragement to write the book and for numerous discussions related to various ideas found in the volume. We are especially indebted to Bill Irvine, Don Pilgrim and Jerry Hackett, who read and commented on the entire manuscript. We sought the advice of Nancy Cartwright, who made substantial comments on Chapter 4. A.W. Coats and A. Russon read a draft of a preliminary paper from which the book developed. Brief comments were also received from Lorie Tarshis, Phillip Mirowski and Brian Bixley.

Lori Scheffel and the editors at Routledge provided valuable assistance with the editing of the text and bibliography and the compiling of the indexes. Finally, we would like to express our appreciation for the helpful and enthusiastic support of our publisher, Alan Jarvis.

Introduction

THE SCOPE OF VERIFICATION IN THIS STUDY

In adopting methods of investigation which are dominated almost exclusively by procedures of assessment in terms of false or true, scholars in many fields have become obsessed with a certain practice of verification employed as a final methodological step, as it were, to screen for error and subjectivity in statements and theories. If indeed all aspects of the world so investigated could be accurately described in terms of black and white and the results of verification so applied would lead to informative conclusions, then the obsession carries no apparent danger. Should it, however, lead to a weakening of the creative formulation of research questions or scholars' reneging in answering questions posed, its influence might rightfully be deemed nefarious. Not surprisingly perhaps, use of an extremely rigid, black-or-white, form of verification by scholars in diverse fields has led to many controversies and disputes among philosophers and discipline methodologists; other logically systematic ways of checking conclusions in an attempt to eliminate error have been subsequently pursued – for example, confirmation, validation or falsification.

In this book the term *verification* is to be understood in a general sense, including every nuance from a strongest (or extreme) form to all weaker means of error elimination by *post facto* consideration. Verification will then broadly mean the procedure by which a scholar's conclusion is related to empirical data for the purpose of establishing either its acceptance (in the strong or weak case – i.e., confirmation), its rejection (falsification) or its modification; verification will thus be considered to encompass 'verification', 'confirmation', 'validation', 'falsification' and 'modification'. It has none the less been found necessary to make a distinction between a 'scientific' positivist form of verifying, in which theories are tested against empirical evidence to establish acceptance or rejection, and a looser form of verifying which does not consist in testing. These two forms of verification are denoted as *Verification A* and *Verification B* respectively.

Beside the two forms of verification of concern here, it ought first to be acknowledged that verification might be understood in yet a third way: *logical verification*, in which the conclusion confirms the theorem which is stated hypothetically. In this case verification falls under the technical form of proof as used in mathematics and of course in a great deal of mathematical economics. This mathematical proof has nothing to do with the notion of verification under consideration here; it is, in fact, methodologically part of model building.

Verification A does pertain here; it consists in testing a theoretical conclusion by empirical evidence, with the result that the conclusion will be established as true or false. Agreement with evidence is the criterion of its falsity or veracity. This rigid and uni-directional conception of verification, referred to throughout this book as Verification A, is that of the neo-positivists. They asserted that it was the only way to establish something as known. It is this understanding of verification that has been adopted by most scholars in quantitative economics and cliometrics.

It is, however, to be suggested in this book that verification can have a decidedly wider and more productive meaning. According to a second pertinent understanding of verification, theoretical conclusions would be conjoined with evidence, yet not with the objective of establishing falsity or veracity. One might speak now of a *Verification B*, in which intermeshing of the theoretical conclusion with empirical evidence would be undertaken in order

1 To permit sense to be made of what are presumed to be regularities and irregularities in the observed world;
2 To find out whether new evidence can help the scholar get a sense of the reliability of the theoretical conclusion; and
3 To affirm that the story suggested is plausible.

The verifying exercise of bringing in evidence becomes a strengthening prolongation of the theory itself; it has nothing to do with testing. In other words, Verification B fosters a reciprocal understanding of a non-definitive theory and changing data about phenomena. Empirical testing in the context of Verification B is meaningless, since evidence cannot fully support any theory, nor can one theory explain all pertinent data as evidence. Given the complexity of societal phenomena and the kinds of facts with which economists and historians deal, ongoing complementing is called for. Its purpose is not to validate a theoretical conclusion, even ultimately, but to improve, complete or revise both the theory (its premises, its arguments or model, maybe even the way the hypothesis is stated) and the empirical data in its form as evidence (documentary, statistical, etc.).

Thus, just as for Verification A, for Verification B, empirical data are not only desirable but imperative. In economics and history, the totality of pertinent empirical data (i.e., every detail, direct and indirect, which could serve as evidence about the phenomena under study) is impossible to attain. To come as close as possible to comprehending the phenomena under study the scholar will, therefore, continuously have to balance and complement the theoretical construct of the phenomena with available data. In so doing, the scholar reveals an awareness of the consequences of the impossibility of obtaining all the evidence, and of the non-sense of using new data as a basis for judging a theory which cannot even present itself as an explanation of all pertinent data. Constant reciprocal complementing of a theory and available, apparently pertinent data will itself provide a more and more precise, and theoretically comprehensive, understanding of phenomena.

VERIFICATION AS AN ISSUE

The practice of verifying has become very widely incorporated in disciplines not traditionally scientific – along the lines, however, of its implementation in the sciences – under two presuppositions. The first is that verification is an appropriate research tool within a particular scholar's discipline. The second is that the results of its application can be interpreted analogously to the way they would be interpreted by a scholar in a pure science. A question one might ask is what is it that has made social scientists and humanists believe that their disciplines can borrow and apply research methods of the sciences to conduct their own research? To what extent is (laboratory) control over situations providing empirical facts, traditionally a mainstay of Verification A in the exact sciences, possible or necessary in the application of Verification A in the disciplines of economics and history?

Scholars in the social sciences and the humanities are, as part of their research procedure, subjecting their findings to Verification A. Their interpretation of Verification A may not, however, necessarily consist in actually observing and scrutinizing closely the world and then comparing a theory's conclusion to it. It might not mean either the subjecting of a conclusion to test by conducting a series of repetitive and similar experiments. Often verification in the disciplines of the social sciences and the humanities consists in using collected data, and further statistical manipulation of it, first to find out whether any correlation exists between the elements (potentially) conjoined by a researcher's conclusion and then to attach a degree of belief or confidence to the findings. Part of the issue then to be raised in the present study on the implications of the use of a verification process at all in economics and history is the manner in which Verification A is conducted and interpreted in the social science and humanities disciplines.

The principal proposition in the book is that economics and history deal with matter as well as human affairs, neither of which can be disassociated from the other through time. Also, despite the fact that these disciplines deal with socio-economic phenomena which do tend to exhibit some general regularities or uniformities for periods of time, such relatively temporary constancies in socio-economic activity behaviour must not be interpreted as reflections of laws resembling those of the exact sciences in permanence. It will be argued that in economics and history important contributions do not rest on the results of approximations extrapolated from apparent regularities, but on an acquired understanding of how various changes take place in the social fabric through the identification and analysis of the forces which could bring about changes. A practice of verification, analogous to that undertaken in the sciences, would become in this context an extremely difficult task, because of both the uni-directional function of the test to check only the theory against unquestioned data, which after all are also another form of abstraction, and the uncontrolled environment in which the test has to be implemented.

Verification as practised in the exact sciences cannot be used as the criterion for confirming or falsifying a theory in economics or history. By way of explaining this assertion, an attempt will be made in the book to answer all the questions raised in this introduction. An explanation of the weaknesses and therefore inappropriateness of the application of the criterion of such a verification will be provided. An alternative approach to verification in the form of a formulation–reformulation step based on a mixture of inductive and deductive reasoning will ultimately be suggested. Closer analysis of the two disciplines will form the point of departure in this introduction.

Why economics and history?

Case studies

The history of education has proved that there are many ways to slice the cake of human knowledge. The philosophy of education or more influentially educative practice has varied extensively in many countries or cultural areas in considering where economics and history belong pedagogically. Three possible groupings have been used: *Geisteswissenschaften*, *sciences humaines* and social sciences–humanities. When economics and history both have traditionally been considered within the same grouping, as in the case of the *Geisteswissenschaften* and *sciences humaines*, some of their common attributes, such as their emphasis on the human creature as *geistreich* or their focus on the aspects of man, his economic behaviour or his record of the past, were deemed the most important ones for grouping them pedagogically. In countries of the Anglo-Saxon heritage, the disciplines of economics and history both may and may not be found within the same grouping; the apron of the social sciences is considered by some educators to include history as well as economics, while others have chosen to retain history's traditional identity as one of the humanities, despite the arrival of the new division of the social sciences.

In any division, it is both the common and distinguishing features of studies that are being emphasized. Whether or not economics and history find themselves both considered social sciences is of some real concern to the question of verification at hand. Undeniably, the social sciences form a disciplinary grouping reflecting the trend of some studies to see themselves as 'sciences of social phenomena'. Clearly those who consciously identify their endeavours as social scientific openly acknowledge the concept of a science as one applicable, to their pedagogy at the very least. It is of course difficult to establish in just what way concepts of science and scientific have been identified from the model of the exact sciences as likewise common currents or would-be features of economics (moral science), political science, psychology, sociology, etc., but without doubt a notion of the testability of research conclusions or the appropriateness of verification has been absorbed.

History is occasionally today found institutionally at home within the disciplinary grouping of the social sciences. While such an attachment may really reflect personal affinities or the physical resources of an institution more than anything else, rhetorical acknowledgement of a possible pedagogical connection between the two betrays an increasing acceptance, if not desire, of many historians to see their study as a science. Traditionally a component of humanities divisions, history is increasingly considered to have flexible affiliations. Its subject matter, if seen as 'the social animal', and a growing methodological interest within the historical circle in quantifiable data reveal that its similarities with the social sciences are more than appearing to increase. This is, therefore, a very interesting moment to examine closely the understanding and use of a notion of verification by historians, for more even than economists, who are already predominantly won over to the scientificity of their discipline, historians may, in deliberating a role for verification, be reflecting their position on the larger question of the appropriateness of their identity, traditionally as humanists, with the sciences.

Thus, to illustrate how verification has been used and interpreted today outside the exact sciences, it seems appropriate to choose economics, of the social sciences, and history, in disciplinary limbo, as exemplary disciplines. Economics is presently the quintessential social science, pushing to realize fully its potential to become 'just like the older (non-social) sciences'. It sees itself as leading the way for other social sciences, as they follow its methodology, to be 'real' sciences as well. From a slightly different perspective, history is also struggling, torn between historians who would like to follow the 'scientific' practices of the social sciences and those who, representing the longer historical tradition, reject such an approach. In confronting these different approaches, historians are shedding light on the importance and appropriateness of empirical investigation methods in the humanities and social sciences in general.

Affinity

Despite the distinctly different foci of economics (activities and things of economic value) and history (the past), the two disciplines share a strong affinity in many respects. Both disciplines have human beings as the principal subjects of their investigation. Both observe, but most importantly analyse, changes in human society and facts of human affairs. For economics this means that the 'keeping track' of economically interesting activities and things within a society is more than an exercise in accounting. Similarly, history's 'narration' of the past is more than a 'blow-by-blow' account of events.

Due to their shared analytic concern with aspects of human activity the disciplines of economics and history face four duals in common in their studies.

1 In each the researcher is an observer of the world but is also intimately a part of it.
2 Each study makes a conceptual distinction between man–nature and man–man relations.
3 The human being, the subject of each discipline, is both passively a spectator and absorber of information and also actively an actor and creator of ideas and decisions.
4 The human activity of interest to each discipline is made up of the interaction between the individual subject and society.

These four duals function as the common backdrop to a further similarity of the studies of economics and history, a common analytic task. The task which both disciplines' scholars have set for themselves is to recognize and explain not simply everyday actions, but more importantly the 'out-of-the-everyday event' and its causes. In each discipline this poses common challenges. Recognizing a crisis might not be difficult for scholars of either discipline, but between the crisis and the quotidian lies a spectrum of 'events' posing the question of their analytic worth. As for the challenge of explaining events by causes, both disciplines are faced with unrepeatable events; (economics is even faced with the as-yet-unrealized ones), and hence ultimately with no way ever to *prove* a cause-and-effect relationship by rerunning them.

To aid them in their analytic task, both economists and historians have adopted one important premise in common: the actions of individuals (at any similar place and time) reflect some regularity. This is assumed in each discipline according to shared ideas about human nature and human communities and systems. Thus, while a slice of human group activity at one place and time is acknowledged by both disciplines to be extremely complex in its dynamics, that intricacy of human activity is also perceived by both disciplines to be understandable if analysed through time. Potential understanding over time is considered possible due to the fact that most changes in human society are gradual. Even in situations of anomalously rapid change, often described as crises, societies have no choice but to adapt according to a continuity between their past and their present forms, however dramatically different they are.

It is the regularity of patterns in human behaviour with their recurrence of certain characteristics and slow change which is seen in both economics and history to make research possible. It affords to both disciplines the possibility of calculating and extrapolating information about past events. It renders neither, however, capable of predicting the future, an assertion which is usually not considered as great a blow to history as it is to economics. Led astray by the powerful tools of statistics, econometrics and computers, economists persist in obliging themselves to be able to predict the future, buoyed by their success with economic indicators such as employment, production or stocks, and ignoring crucial evidence of the vainness of the soothsayers' endeavour in the crisis of 1929, in the consequences of economic changes at the end of the Second World War, in the 1971 dollar crisis, the oil crises, the unexpected and unprecedented rise in interest rates in 1980–2, or in the stock exchange crash of 1987. Both disciplines could do worse than to stress their affinity, limited as it may be, simply to understand the past and present better and to hold informed ideas based on their research of what to expect in the future, without claiming to be able to predict it.

Why verification?

Appeal to verification in economics and history

Publications in virtually every major professional journal of economics and history, and especially in those of applied economics, show that a great deal of research involves econometrics, cliometrics or some kind of statistical study manipulating data. Many publications include empirical studies and offer some form of test of their conclusions. The appeal to verification through statistical testing and data manipulation is becoming so routine that increasingly among applied economists and applied historians such 'black-box' techniques are in widespread, unquestioned use. The majority is persuaded that such practices indeed constitute truly empirical investigations. It is in opposition to this narrow belief that the issues in the present book are addressed.

Methodological and philosophical issue

In the present study verification is to be treated both in terms of its function as a methodological procedure and as a philosophical notion. Although economists and historians need not differ in philosophical persuasions to find themselves divided on the implementation of verification within their methodologies, they are very likely to find themselves at odds if the ontological and epistemological premises of their respective disciplines are not shared. The status of verification in methodological and philosophical discussions has varied over time. While in antiquity it was one important step among several in the inquiry after knowledge, its role during the medieval period seems to have diminished as theories concerning logical, metaphysical or theological issues using *a priori* reasoning dominated. It was only later, when science and scientific investigation again became the epistemological model for most disciplines, that verification regained a privileged status.

Verification found its first advocate in Aristotle and its first home in the study of the natural world, the physics of antiquity. Ever since the classical emphasis on the enquiry into fundamental change and constancy in the physical world, physics has dominated as the model of an intellectual endeavour. Further, as physics came to deal specifically with the sensible aspects of earth's natural world, its researchers began to employ experimental techniques both to discover new features and to test their hypotheses about others already observed. Many of Aristotle's epistemological and pedagogical assumptions and his ontological conclusions about physical things survived the restriction in the focus of the study of physics. Each type of assumption left a legacy of importance to the notion and use of verification: that human beings come to know things through sense experience, that there are essential aspects of physical things which are a part of their every instance, and, the very important legacy of Aristotelian teleology, that some form of recomparing newly acquired knowledge with the investigated objects is a part of 'scientific' investigation.

Long after Aristotle the sciences are still enjoying an exonerated status, through their apparently rigorous, precise, unified theories and useful conclusions. Looking for the recipe to such an enviable position of intellectual respect, researchers in numerous disciplines seem to have persuaded themselves that science's theoretical constructs and fruitful results are the result of a 'scientific method'. For their studies to reach the status of the sciences then, all they assumed they would have to do is to follow the same methodology. Thus, along with attempts at the adoption of experimentation (preferably controlled and repeatable) and mathematics, researchers have tried to incorporate a form of verification derived from the sciences. To conduct an investigation worthy of the name 'scientific' has come therefore in part to imply the subjecting of one's findings to verification.

Ought economists and historians to look to the sciences as intellectually exonerate and follow in the footsteps of those researchers who adopt from their methodologies? Is such a transfer of investigative approaches possible? The general attitude is yes. But is it, in fact, simply methodology which lies at the heart of the differences between physics, and economics and history and the apparent merit of their respective conclusions? Indeed economists and historians can and probably ought to subject their theoretical conclusions to some form of test. In the present book it will be argued, however, that with the human being as the prime subject matter of economics and history and the involuntary involvement of the researcher the stage is preset for economists and historians to face very different kinds of studies from those of the sciences. To work on this stage demands a methodology whose components are specifically designed as distinct from those of the sciences. From it will ensue a very different epistemological and ontological result.

In this book, a brief history of the scientifization of economics and history will be surveyed. Then the concept of verification as it pertains to economics and history, its use and the problems it raises will be discussed. A great deal of emphasis will be put on individual decisions and actions as an important component of the studies of economics and history. The interactions between individuals will be extensively developed. Finally, it will be argued that in economics and history establishing correlations between phenomena is equivalent neither to formulating nor to verifying theories about them. Our understanding of theory formulation and verification requires an acknowledgement of causal relations which in the case of the dynamics of the individual and of groups, and hence of their abstractions in economics and history, is not necessarily deterministic.

It will be presented in Chapter 1 how, in the last 300 years, the disciplines of economics and history have slowly undergone a move toward scientifization. There will also be an explanation of the meaning of 'scientific' and 'scientific method' will be presented. It will be argued that the move toward scientifization can be viewed as an improvement in the manner in which sources are to be utilized as well as in the way premises and theories are to be conceived and assessed in order to diminish scholars' *a priori* biases and value judgements. None the less, under the strong influence of the neo- positivism which still persists today in economics and history, the increasing and excessive reliance on facts, meaning data, as the ultimate resort for judging whether a theory is accepted or rejected has led to an awkward and rigid conception of verification (Verification A), which is not a proper verification *per se*.

It will be explained in Chapter 2 how fact, theory and verification are understood in economics and history. It will then be shown how facts are taken for granted as neutral and scientific, although the choice of them as data is itself simply an extension and reflection of theoretical premises. This is especially acute when they are used as the empirical support in the verification of theories. In fact, independent of the degree of formalization and the process of verification, theoretical premises and the choice of important variables in economics and history often reflect scholars' personal involvement and are made according to value judgements. It is recognized that because of the nature of economic and historical phenomena in which societal interactions are involved there are tremendous difficulties in conceptualizing such phenomena. Due to a number of limitations – such as incompleteness, ignorance, complexity of interdependences, etc. – at each stage in the theorizing process simplifications, complications and even distortions are introduced, gradually transforming the actual phenomena under study into an abstract configuration. The ensuing theories are about abstract phenomena. With Verification A as the test of the theory against evidence in the form of abstract data, a return to the actual phenomena is impossible. An unfortunate side effect of the scientifization by appeal to Verification A is the belief that economics and history are positive sciences. In fact, most positive statements in economics and history contain normative content. It is not surprising that polarization into different schools of thought persists in the two disciplines.

It is apparent that the study of phenomena of interest to economics and history cannot be reduced simply to phenomena of nature. There will be in Chapter 3 a discussion of the implications of the above-mentioned four duals as common characteristics of both economics and history: observer and participant, human and non-human, passivity and activity of the individual, and the individual and the group. It will be explained how, for separate reasons, the duals undermine three conditions which some scholars consider essential to the ability to study their subject matter: a detached objectivity of the researcher, the ability to observe all conditions which are theoretically potential causes of an outcome, and the ability to set up a control observation environment. Much attention will be given to a far subtler implication of the duals – their impact on the regular occurrence of events under scrutiny in economics and history. For, while regularity of phenomena allows the easiest access to understanding them, within these duals lie the seeds of indecipherable irregularity.

In Chapter 4 it is going to be argued that a discussion of verification is closely related to one of causality. Much attention, thus, has to be given to the issue of causality in economics or history. Recognition of the particularities of causality in the two disciplines is very significant, especially as their desired scientificity increases. In the sciences it is well appreciated that it is only in cases where deterministic causal relations can be established that Verification A can be employed to reasonable effect. Most of the forces which are the causes of economic and historical perturbations over time are not deterministic, despite the fact that some general characteristics may appear to reccur. Thus, if a practice of verification is restricted to instances of deterministic causality its application will not only be limited to specific theories, but its role and contribution will be sorely reduced.

It will be asserted that a more flexible notion of verification (Verification B) can be, and has to be, introduced. Any theory, or 'story' of posited causal relations, is subject to verification, or a 'test' of plausibility. In the sciences, plausibility of a theory is in large part based on the assertion that 'test will reveal that the posited causal connections constantly hold true because their effects are consistently producable as predicted'. In the case of economics and history it is suggested that testing is not feasible and that the premise on which such tests might prove valuable does not apply in the two disciplines.

In the Conclusion ('A sequel to scientifization') it will be suggested that when, however, a theory is not subjected to testing but is constantly undergoing reinterpretation and reformulation through exposure to new facts it means that the process of verification is no longer a judgemental assessment. It does not even now make sense to speak of 'the' initial theory as a good one or not. Instead, one must speak of the theory as a mutable set of ideas which as a recognizable unity is subject to change. A theory will be deemed to be sound if, over the course of ongoing interpretation, it continues to demonstrate stability.

Chapter 1

The history of the notion of verification

In the last 300 years, partly under the influence of changes in the physical sciences, philosophy and the philosophy of science, and partly as a result of their own evolution, the disciplines of economics and history have gradually come to be 'scientifized'. Scientifization, as will be explained, has come to mean that precision is valued in articulating ideas and concepts, and that explanations are to be asserted on the basis of logic and/or empirical evidence, not on supranatural or mystical considerations. Assertions which are based on belief or simple narration have become increasingly denigrated in economics and history, as they have been in the sciences, as insufficient for reliable knowledge. Thus the process of scientifization has undoubtedly provided an improvement in the manner in which phenomena of economic and historical interest are investigated; it has, however, at the same time, also created an inferiority complex in many economists and some historians,[1] who understand scientifization to mean that economics and history should be concerned with the study of matter in a fashion similar to the exact sciences, especially physics, and that the *only* approach to rigorous and value-free analysis is quantitative methods.[2] Economists and historians manifest their inferiority complex in their attempts to copy and apply (or to combat zealously the analogy to) the method of pre-twentieth-century physics, instead of concentrating on developing modes of investigation proper to the problems of their disciplines.

As part of the scientifizing of economics and history, premises based on observations and facts, and conclusions to be compared with empirical evidence have become indispensable in the process of investigation. Almost inevitable has been the attempt to employ a rigid notion of verification, 'Verification A', and to carry it out in a way similar to that used in physics as its criterion for validating or falsifying a theory.

It will be argued in this chapter that the scientifization of research methodologies which started centuries ago has not belonged exclusively to the physical sciences, but has been shared by the disciplines of economics and history, among others. Scientifization is not understood here to mean necessarily the exclusive use of quantitative methods.[3] Scientifization of economics and history has resulted primarily from:

1 An interest in generalities about aspects of the world they study;
2 An increasing awareness of the need for rigorous analysis, consisting of logical argumentation in addition to hypotheses and founded premises, to lead to the asserting of a generality;
3 Importance placed on the role of observation, documentary evidence and facts in establishing reliable knowledge.

The obtaining of knowledge of generalities through logical analysis requires a scientific methodology which, it is argued, must include a notion of verification. A conception of 'scientific' method that is no more appropriate to physics than it is to economics or history will be proposed. This conception does not necessitate that the subject matter of economics or history resemble that of physics or astronomy any further than that each admit of regularities; nor does it necessitate the use of quantitative methods. It will be advanced that since the affirming of knowledge about empirical situations is an important part of the disciplines of economics and history, a significant step then of their scientific methodology will consist in bringing together theories and their conclusions with facts. It is proposed that the method of Verification B, broader than that of Verification A, is the only legitimate way of bringing together conclusions and facts in economics and history.

A short chronological survey of the gradual scientifization of economics and history, as well as the increasing importance of verification within that scientifization, will include in brief:

1 The rise of positivism in the nineteenth century and the state of methodology in economics and history toward the end of the century;
2 The distinction between *a priori* and empiricist epistemologies of the eighteenth and nineteenth centuries and how each affected economists and historians of the same period;
3 The ways in which the neo-positivism of the 1920s affected both

economics and history with its new, rigid attitude toward the concept of verification; and, finally,

4 The post-war state of methodology in both disciplines.

Most recently, a large number of economists seem to have accepted the techniques of statistics and mathematical probability as the appropriate tools for verifying theoretical conclusions and predicting future events. Meanwhile, it fortunately cannot be said that the new quantitative methods have as yet become as much a part of history's general methodology, let alone of its verification step. The relatively small number of historians who became caught up in cliometrics at its outset in the early 1960s elicited sharp criticism from a large portion of the historical profession, and a bitter methodological dispute has ensued (Davis and Engerman 1987). Any controversy surrounding the techniques of statistics and probability seems in economics, as in history, to have focused not on the appropriateness of using verification as conceived nor on its present role, but on the procedures for verifying.

THE LEVEL OF AWARENESS OF THE METHODOLOGICAL ISSUES IN ECONOMICS AND HISTORY

Only sporadically in economics and history have the foundations of the disciplines' methodologies and the methodologies themselves been of major interest or concern. Indeed there have always been individual authors who, independent of the current fashionable focus of their discipline, have made their main contributions in the area of methodology. It could not, however, be said that methodology has consistently been a strong concern in the two disciplines at large. In the nineteenth century, however, there were notable economists and historians (for example, Senior, Mill, Jevons, Walras, von Ranke, Marx, Hegel) who in devoting considerable attention to the subject matter of their disciplines came consequently to address explicitly the question of proper method and implicitly the philosophical premises underlying it. By the end of the century, specific schools of economic and historical study identifiable by their methodological differences had quite purposefully established themselves.[4]

In the nineteenth century, although some specific methodological schools of economic and historical study (e.g. New Historical School) expanded in number, the demarcation lines between each one remained quite fixed until well into the twentieth century. An interest in shared methodological concerns remained until recently almost non-existent. This can be said despite the appearance of a few isolated works, such as those of Hutchison (1938) and Machlup (1955) in economics and Weber (1949) and Collingwood (1946) in history. Aside from their efforts, the primary locus of any methodological consideration was for economists the short essay[5] and for historians the preface of the historical work. These expositions, however, provided the justification of the individual scholar's method of approach rather than a long and deep reflection on the philosophical and methodological posture proposed.

In economics, it took a realization, in the 1960s and 1970s, of the changed state of the discipline (that it had become increasingly mathematically technical, increasingly reliant on complex statistical modes of empirical investigation, and increasingly weak in its ability to anticipate events) to cause fundamental questions of methodology to be raised anew and widely.[6] Since then, in response, whole groups of economists have arisen whose main interest is methodology; their teaching and research now form a sub-discipline, economic method. At about the same time, in history, on the other hand, both a slow realization that the world of the past had changed dramatically and that other disciplines might provide new ways of describing such changes, rendered methodology topical once again. Of great appeal to a small group of historians in the 1960s, identifying themselves as cliometricians (with an eye to the model of econometricians), was the potential insight the infusion of mathematics into history's methodology might yield.[7] Resistance from other historians who remain sceptical about the appropriateness of such new social scientific practices has presently fuelled in history a most lively methodological debate.

When methodological issues in economics and history were of concern, both most recently and at times much more removed, they often focused to some degree on the notion of the 'scientific' as it pertains to them. The disciplines' understanding of this notion and its companion, scientific method are crucial to understanding the notion and role of verification in the two disciplines. Increasing emphasis on verification, particularly Verification A, in economics and history has gone hand-in-hand with an increasing scientifization of the disciplines. A discussion of the notion of 'scientific' and of scientific methodology will help establish why this is the case. A subsequent chronological analysis will demonstrate that it is the case.

PROGRESSIVE SCIENTIFIZATION OF THE DISCIPLINES AND ITS RAMIFICATIONS FOR A NOTION OF VERIFICATION

The notion of 'scientific'

The word 'science' is derived from the Latin term, *scientia*, meaning knowledge. Each Latin writer who used the word implied ontological and epistemological conclusions about what is 'knowable' and how we can come to have 'knowledge' about it. Such conclusions determined whether a field of discussion could or could not be considered a science and, more importantly perhaps, the degree to which the subject matter in question and the human inquiry of it render it 'knowable'. Different ontological and epistemological conceptions of the world lead to differing definitions of a science and hence to different conclusions about the possible claims to science of an area of study.

Since antiquity, the notion of science appears to have become quite restrictive, embracing now only specific areas of object investigation undertaken in a specific way. Actually, however, modern use of the term science simply glosses over, for the most part, the underlying important, specifying assumptions it implies about 'knowledge' and the 'knowable'. In general parlance, what science is seems to be easily understood (in part because not all knowledge is thought to be scientific and not all scholars scientists). It might thus at first appear reasonable to assume that scientists are defined either philosophically, by the fact that they all share a specific philosophical posture (about what science and scientific are), and/or pragmatically, by the fact that they go about doing what they do quite differently from the way non-scientists do what they do. Today's science is, however, not tightly definable by exclusive philosophical convictions or practices, but falls instead within certain wider, inclusive bounds of identity. The widest bounds of 'science' can be specified both ontologically and epistemologically.

Since antiquity a 'science' has been defined as a discipline composed of things 'known' and having a method of investigation which allows for more things to become 'known'. Thus, for a discipline to be scientific it must have a subject matter which is ontologically and epistemologically accessible to being 'known'. First, this means that the subject matter of a science must act in accordance with some form of regularity (i.e. with its instances recurring in time, in place, in like fashion or type, etc.). Second, the study must set out to 'know' and have a way to 'come to know' the generalities and patterns, or perhaps even the laws, which pertain to the existence and activity of its subject matter. If a discipline is a science whose practitioners 'seek to know' and are able to 'come to know' generalities, or laws, which do exist and which might be specifically pertinent to its subject matter, the question is whether or not economics and history are scientific disciplines.

On scientific method

A conviction in the 'scientific knowability' (as opposed to the 'religious knowability' or 'poetic/rhetorical knowability') of a thing derives from two epistemological premises:

1 That 'if a thing is "now" when I examine it just as it was "then" when I last conceived or examined it and this is consistently the case, then I "know" what it is'; and
2 That 'if the thing can show itself as "what it is" consistently to us, then in time we will be able to learn (or will have learned) "what it is"'.

It is then the regularity of the existence and activity of the thing which renders it 'reliably knowable' and without which human beings would not be able to 'know' that they 'know' it. Quite convinced by some degree of ontological regularity, that there are 'scientifically knowable' things, human beings have tried to create a best way for going about knowing them. The ways which were or are thought to help in the acquiring of 'scientific knowledge' might be identified as 'scientific' methods. There has been much discussion about the scientific method (its origins, the specifics of its application, etc.), most of which is not of concern; the object here is to establish the widest bounds inside which a discipline might be deemed to be undertaking its study methodologically 'scientifically'.

The single most important component, and a *sine qua non*, of 'scientific knowability' and hence of a scientific methodology is verification. Verification is the methodological step in which the thing conceived or examined 'then' is re-examined 'now'. If the thing when re-examined is seen to be what it was when last conceived or examined then its existence and activity are deemed to be regular and 'known'. The belief that new knowledge has been acquired seems supported. Thus with each new verification, conviction in the two essential epistemological premises underlying 'scientific knowledge' is reaffirmed.

In order to appreciate the riveting importance of verification within a scientific method one must examine the other essential components common to all versions of the method:

1 Premises;
2 Hypothesis;
3 Arguments or model;
4 Theoretical conclusion; and
5 Verification.

These components comprise the methodological building blocks of a theory.[8]

1 Premises are the starting point for the method and the theory, setting out the initial assumptions (for example, people are greedy, or people like war), whose content is based on *a priori* and/or *a posteriori* knowledge, and for whose acceptance the 'scientist' has no intention of arguing within this application of the method.
2 An hypothesis is an assessment of the state of the thing under theoretical investigation; it may be presented as a plausible cause–effect relationship.
3 The arguments, or model, represent the necessary formal links between the elements or variables which the hypothesis draws into consideration by the theory; they can be constructed syllogistically, through deductive reasoning from premises or inductive inference from empirical evidence, or analogically, and formalized in mathematical terms, symbolic logic, or codified terminology or symbols.
4 The conclusion is the determined imperative theoretical result of the arguments' or model's representation of the hypothesis.[9]
5 Verification is the comparison of the thing 'now' with the thing as presented in the theoretical conclusion 'then'. It is the attempt to establish a relationship between the theoretical conclusion of the model and part of the world it describes.

If a study is to provide reliable knowledge then a general coherent method is required. Steps 1–4 establish the conclusion. That product is then the theoretical assessment of the postulated hypothesis as credible. To proceed, its form is presented for verification. Step 5, verification, establishes the basis for a conclusion to be considered a statement of potentially knowable scientific knowledge. It will be argued in Chapters 2 and 4 that the conception of Verification A is at odds with the potential of the 'scientific' methodology to perform as a coherent method and to fulfil its aim to yield knowledge.

The five steps entail a scientific method, regardless of whether each step contains observable or non-observable, measurable or non-measurable, qualitative or quantitative, determinist or probabilistic elements. The scientification of any discipline is determined fundamentally by whether or not it uses the five-step method. Its degree of scientification is far more nuanced. It will, by the same token, not depend on the number of steps it uses (since it either does or does not employ the whole method), but rather on the degree of rigour in the articulation of its concepts, the internal logical consistency of its statements and the links which draw together its arguments, and its commitment to translating and interpreting theoretical terms into the language of observation. Mathematical formalization is only one form of expression, however powerful; though often taken to be, it is not the exclusive criterion for assessing 'scientification'.

Very early in the scientification of economics and history the debate arose as to whether the disciplines could be defined purely as 'sciences' or whether they should be qualified as 'social sciences', 'moral sciences', 'human sciences', 'mental sciences', etc.[10] The term, 'science' kept reappearing. Although the course of scientification of the two disciplines was revealing a move away from general assertions based on mere belief and the narration of past events based on partisan or glorifying impressions to conclusions based on a 'critical examination of the evidence', under discussion was not whether economics and history could ontologically be considered sciences, but rather what 'kind of sciences' they really were. Confusion arose with attempts to answer the question by means of a distortive analogy to the ideals of astronomy or physics.[11]

Reflecting a new methodological concern, the question was really meant significantly to be about the ways in which economics, history, physics and astronomy apply a method of scientific investigation. The real issue lies then in (the openness or restrictiveness of) the application of a method considered suited to the discipline's inquiry. According to one interpretation, it might be deemed necessary for there to be a simple relation between each component of the theory and each step of the research method.[12] If this is a one-to-one correspondence the verified result of the theoretical inquiry will be unique and definite, as in many instances of concern to physics. It is, in fact, only in this way that a theoretical law can be deemed to be established.[13]

Another interpretation of a possible scientific theory–method relation would stipulate the simplification of a situation acknowledged as complex in which, for example, the subject of investigation is not really extrapolatable from its context, and fruitful application of the method is difficult, or impossible to assess (Shackle 1972). In such an instance the choice of elements considered within the theory (which may in fact still propose a one-to-one correspondence, albeit successively or dialectically) is discretionary or admittedly tentative. The outcome of the application of scientific methodology to a theory is in this case a conditional result. Many areas of investigation in economics and history are considered to require this way of applying the method. Consequently, many of their scientifically established results are of the conditional variety.

Before leaving the idea of distinguishing 'kinds of sciences' entirely, however, let us note that the expression seems to have a continuing usefulness in one realm of distinctions. It seems that while all sciences must presuppose the regularity of the phenomena which concern them, not all sciences must consider the description of that regularity the be all and end all of their study. In fact, it is along the line of this emphasis on regularity that the 'sciences' seem to divide themselves into two kinds. There is a first kind, for whom regularities are the primary focus. A second kind uses regularities as the backdrop against which its primary concern, the 'irregular event' stands out.

The pure sciences, such as physics and chemistry are sciences of the first kind. They concentrate on detecting down to the finest detail the regularity of phenomena and on expressing that regularity by adherence to law. In this kind of science, irregularities are merely such in appearance and play the role of 'ticklers', or guides in the 'scientist's' search for an underlying profound regularity of which anomalies are a 'regular' part. Sciences of the second kind acknowledge the experience of true irregularities and extreme infrequencies; such 'events' are made the primary focus of their study. Both economics and history are of this second kind of science, as is perhaps political science.[14]

HISTORICAL APPROACHES TO METHOD

Positivism and economics and history

As the use of the scientific method increases among economists and historians, these scholars continue to be divided on the method-ological issue of how to employ it well. This is perhaps not surprising, since bits and pieces essential for the application of the scientific method to economics and history can be said to have existed since the beginning of the study of human history and economic activity, and especially from the time each study became recognized as a professional endeavour or discipline.[15] One might assume that the long history of historical writing would have, at least, offered to historians sufficient time and experience to collect the bits and pieces necessary for a consistently practicable method, and long before the young discipline of modern economics began groping for the recipe. It is indeed true that some exemplarily methodological historians existed as long ago as ancient Greece: Herodotus and Thucydides, who recognized the historian's responsibility of making a reliable record of the past available to those who would follow, Polybius who provided a model for the use of *a priori* concepts concerning the regularity of human activity in a theoretical combination with empirical information, and the Roman Livy, who in the first century B.C. demonstrated that generalizations could be recognized as 'too sweeping' and in need of qualification. In addition, with general agreement about the past (and the present which is deemed worthy of memory in the future) as the subject matter of historical study and an almost constantly present spirit of inquiry, it is perhaps even more difficult to see what was in fact missing in the methodology of history to render it 'scientific'.

It seems that until relatively recently both history and economics lacked conviction in the overwhelming appropriateness of a rigorous inductive process in the investigation of their subjects. Indeed its appropriateness was not completely obvious,[16] for, among other reasons, there is the one that two logical processes of investigation present themselves to any inquiring scholar. An inductive process offers a way of arriving at a theoretical conclusion based on generalizing from particular observed or documented instances. A deductive process, however, commends reasoning, ostensibly quite independently of empirical inspiration, from general premises to non-contradicting exemplifying instances. Ever since the conception of the two methods the induction–deduction distinctions have led to complicated epistemological debates; they have periodically divided philosophers, but economists and historians as well, into separate camps.

The inductive logical system of positivism was ultimately to become the essential model for twentieth-century scientifizing. Not surprisingly perhaps it still continues to be most appealing to the 'scientists' among the disciplines of economics and history. By the 1920s the two disciplines had so embraced positivism that they had prepared a very fertile bed for neo-positivist culture. Each discipline had embraced the importance of: empirically inspired (*a priori*) premises, derived from other disciplines as hypothetical or conclusive; mathematical and statistical methods for establishing correspondence between empirical phenomena and logical constructs; analysis focused on what was deemed an empirically isolatable entity; and acknowledging any regularity of the phenomena under study. Each one of these played an important part in forming the present notion of Verification A as practised in economics and cliometrics.

In very few words the economist Jevons captured the essence of his discipline before it received neo-positivism:

> its ultimate laws are known to us immediately by intuition, or, at any rate, they are furnished to us ready made by other mental or physical sciences. That every person will choose the greater apparent good; that human wants are more or less quickly satiated; that prolonged labour becomes more and more painful, are a few of the simple inductions on which we can proceed to reason deductively with great confidence. From these axioms we can deduce the laws of supply and demand, the laws of that difficult conception, value, and all the intricate results of commerce, so far as data are available. The final agreement of our inferences with *a posteriori* observations ratifies our method.
>
> (Jevons 1871: 18).

Indeed, a large portion of the dominant school of economics proceeded into the early twentieth century with great confidence in its foundations. Although the body of its axiomatic premises had grown and was accompanied by ever more general and particular hypothetical premises, either the 'truth' value or the logical value of these premises had come to be accepted, in fact taken for granted, by the 1920s. Many of those that became premises of convention would have far-reaching implications for theory-building and verifying. Some, such as *ceteris paribus*, exacted simplification, and reduction thus began to be undertaken in theorizing.

As for statistics, by the early twentieth century a wide spectrum of economists, such as Jevons, Edgeworth, Bowley and Keynes, and some historians as well, such as G. Lefebvre, had already explored important aspects of statistics and probability. Meanwhile, the study of pure statistics was itself progressing rapidly. R. A. Fisher was exploring probability evidential, J. Neyman and E. S. Pearson introduced procedures for testing hypotheses which stressed probability as an element in decision-making, and the basic concept of stochastic processes introduced by the Russian mathematicians Kitchine and Kolmogorov were to transform radically probability mathematics in the early 1930s (Wegman 1986).

Economists and historians kept abreast of the novelties and ways of integrating statistical concepts and techniques. By the 1940s developments in statistics, probability and in many areas of mathematics, such as linear programming, were so enthusiastically embraced within economics that they brought about wholly new sub-disciplines, econometrics and quantitative economics. In history, adoption of statistical methods also eventually created a completely new brand of historian, the cliometrician, for whom the application of statistical methods (mostly those already dry-run by econometricians) was considered part of plying the trade. Statistics continued into the post-war era to receive high praise as a useful research method in both economics and history. In history, statistics had come to be considered by some as invaluable to studies of the activity and mindset of the collective, as a single entity as well as to some prosopographic and demographic studies of the discrete elements of a whole.

> Unless we resort to statistical method as our primary instrument, collective life cannot be deciphered. . . . Statistics is essential for the determination of values, fortunes, and mentalities; unless these matters are approached through a minute analysis of prices, salaries, political trends, and cultural tendencies, it is possible to understand nothing.
>
> (J.L. Vives, in Gay and Wexler 1972: vol. 4, 217)[17]

As practice testifies, in the economics of the early twentieth century the importance of statistics was certainly not being denied, though it too had its share of dissenters.[18]

By the early twentieth century both economics and history had also evolved to the point of isolating, conceptually if not mathematically, the items under discussion within their studies. Since their beginnings, each discipline had had groups of scholars which either placed emphasis on the composite entity (the state, the firm, etc.), or gave their full attention to the individual *per se*. By the 1920s, holism and individualism had both found strongly antagonistic advocates in each discipline.[19] Vociferous advocacy of particular conceptually distinct entities as most appropriate for study led to the fractioning of each discipline into subdisciplines. Classical political economy became separated into economics, with the individual primarily as its subject, and sociology, with the composite entity society as its focus. The history of economics drifted away from both divisions. History also began to partition, at first into one group of historians whose attention focused on groups of people and societies and another persistently adhering to the traditional 'great man/woman' history, with its emphasis on individuals of prominence.

Ideological, rather than methodological, grounds determined in many cases a scholar's choice of subject and hence of new discipline. Since each economic or historical study considered its entities discrete, scholars of whatever stripe were indeed unified in their readiness for neo-positivism and its Verification A. By the 1920s, however, methodological premises of holism or individualism were set up and in the post-neo-positivist era the wedge between individualism and holism has become increasingly due to methodological differences. This has indeed created further partitioning between and within the disciplines of economics and history. In both, however, individualists and holists continue to be pegged, or to peg themselves, to ideologies (for example, individualists to free market and *laissez-faire* ideology, holists to Marxism).

Among the new disciplines sociology began immediately to consider its separation in terms of methodology. It was asked, for example, how concepts of causality would pertain to a study of society and its component collective elements. Sociology conceived explanations of social activity as dependent on cultural, political and institutional as well as economic factors. In the context of the multitude of causes effecting social events, the existence of social regularities and even laws came to be posited.

The type of social science in which we are interested is an *empirical science* of concrete *reality* (*Wirklichkeitswissenschaft*). . . . The "laws" which we are able to perceive in the infinitely manyfold stream of events must – according to this conception – contain the scientifically "essential" aspect of reality . . . . Even among the followers of the Historical School we continually find the attitude which declares that the ideal which all the sciences, including the cultural sciences, serve and towards which they should strive even in the remote future is a system of propositions from which reality can be "deduced".

(Weber 1949: 100–1)

Sociology, and particularly Weber's concept of a social science, have had an undeniable effect on economics and history. In the case of either discipline, any scholar's conviction today in the existence of social laws is largely due to Weber (and Marx). For historians, adoption of the "generalizing" approach of the social sciences' meant rejection of the 'individualizing' of historicism, and many historians[20] willingly accepted the trade-off for the gain of a concept of social laws.[21] Oftimes, however, they added their own qualifiers as to what constituted historical social law. Lefebvre, for example, while seeking for laws realized that the best he could hope to establish were 'constants', with no value for prediction.

Economics and history had thus by the 1920s embraced the positivist importance of acknowledged regularity in phenomena, analysis of the isolatable entity, mathematical and statistical methods, and empirically inspired premises. Yet other factors also rendered them susceptible to neo-positivist scientificity, and more of their scientification process deserves mention, however briefly. From the beginnings in the nineteenth century of professional economics and history until well into the twentieth century, the two disciplines have shown themselves eager to carry on the legacy of much earlier forms of *a priori* and empirical reasoning. They have also been, and continue to be, influenced by the current forms of those and other epistemological ideas. Of special interest here is the reflection of that influence in the disciplines' conception of a proper method, and particularly in their attitude toward the roles of observation and verification.

A priorism and empiricism

From their beginnings, economics and history have vacillated between the two logical approaches to theoretical analysis: induction and deduction. For each, two sufficiently representative groups of influential partisan philosophers can be identified: the classical *a priori* group which ran from Plato to Descartes, Leibniz, and Kant; and the empiricists dominated especially by the English philosophers Bacon, Hobbes, Locke, Berkley and Hume. The philosophical aim of the *a priori* school was to favour, in varying degrees, logical premises and reasoning based on them, at the epistemological expense of using experience acquired though the senses. For extreme empiricists, on the other hand, the mind could entertain no ideas other than those derived from experience through the senses. Although no economist nor historian today denies the value of observations, predominant sympathy with one philosophical school of theory-building logic or the another continues to determine to a great degree both how important the scholar considers empirical evidence in the scientific method to be and with what degree of philosophical verve empirical evidence is used. It is of particular importance to note here that verification, as the last step of the scientific method, and its use of observation are far more appealing to empiricists than to *a priori* advocates.

Historically, *a priori* philosophers have considered knowledge obtainable by deduction from *a priori* ideas and have been concerned with philosophy in the broadest sense, thus, as including theological as well as metaphysical issues. Laws of nature, they have argued, are primarily discovered through mental reasoning; most such philosophers have, however, added that this does not exclude the use of evidence provided by experience or observation. According to believers in empiricism, on the other hand, knowledge is not deduced from *a priori* ideas but obtained through induction from experience and facts. The tremendous advance in the natural sciences and classical mechanics in the sixteenth and seventeenth century, triggered by Galileo's, Kepler's and Newton's theories and empirical investigations, certainly tickled the mind of philosophers as to the role of observation. It is not surprising that the rise of empiricism, which crystallized in Hume's notion of causality (that the perception of a succession of events as causes and effects stems from experience and observation), took place during this period.

By the mid-eighteenth century, economists and historians

reflected a certain awareness of deductive philosophy, specifically of Cartesianism, in setting out general propositions to reach conclusions about hypotheses.[22] The French Physiocrat economist, Quesnay, drawing on patterns of organic life to understand issues of economic life, did in fact produce *a priori* a theory of surplus (*Tableau économique*), on which much Marxist theory was later built. His original definitions of 'surplus' and 'production' led him to conclude that only the agricultural sector of a society's economy is 'productive' and, hence, to assert that the state's full fiscal burden should fall on its farmers. Such conclusions were subsequently ridiculed as 'detrimental' and 'unfounded', and the whole *a priori* process was denigrated (Say 1880: xxxiv).[23] There also exist, by the same token, examples of other prominent eighteenth-century intellectuals whose application of *a priori* reasoning to economic issues have remained untarnished: Turgot's (1767) deduced 'law of diminishing return of a factor' continues to be accepted as an *a priori* established axiom in economics today.

Writers of history pursued *a priori* methods of analysis far less fruitfully in the mid-eighteenth century than did their contemporary writers on economic activity. The Cartesian tradition, which has been characterized as having 'little use for history' (Gay and Cavanaugh 1972: vol. 1, xix), indeed offered little by way of guidelines for a critical historical posture. Instead, the *a priori* method, which had been employed in Christian polemics since Augustine of Hippo, became an equally captive rhetorical tool of the opposing anti-Christian polemicists of the Enlightenment. The *a priori* method flourished uncritically, with a few remarkable exceptions such as the work of Voltaire and Gibbon, as 'theories of universal and uniform human nature directed the attention of eighteenth-century historians to what men had in common rather than what divided them and made them unique' (Gay and Cavanaugh 1972: vol. 1 xix). While the ground had been prepared for an emphasis on sound empirical evidence and the inductive method there are few indications that the two components had been previously methodologically combined.

In eighteenth-century history it would take a different philosophical thrust articulated by the critical historian–philosopher Hume to give strength to the seeds for profound methodological changes. Hume found prominence in his own day from his historical rather than his philosophical writings. As, however, his history was in effect his philosophy applied, he exercised immediate influence on historians undeniably both as philosopher and model historian. Hume's predecessors in spirit, Valla, Bodin and especially Mabillon, had already formulated and practised critical attitudes towards the use of documentary evidence in the writing of history, respectively by rooting out forged documents, assessing the work of other historians, and setting down a whole method of diplomatics. Bacon, while emphasizing a clear distinction between the writing of history and the search for its documentation, none the less equally pointedly advocated the study of the world's past by the inductive method from sources already to hand.

With his synthetic understanding of the use of evidence and the inductive method, Hume was to deflate at least temporarily an issue consciously troubling some historians about the possibility of a firm historical methodology. The *trattatisti* of the sixteenth century had tackled 'the problem of *electio*' or 'the way to select properly the important data from among the infinite number of past events' (Breisach 1983: 189). Their initial concern was to be assuaged, on the one hand, by a belief in the availability of ultimate Truth (if not in history's conclusions), then in God's message, and by a sense of the pedagogical adequacy of the moral conclusions historians had drawn over time.[24] On the other hand, an attempt to itemize all the possible causes of an effect (for example, the list of all possible human motives by Patrizi), seemed to offer a way of evaluating or sorting the choices for what might be 'the important data'. Hume acknowledged the difficulties of *electio*, but, none the less, imbued documentary evidence with the full privilege of permitting the establishing of first causes for effects under discussion.

Hume's 'constructive scepticism' offered the doubting scholar in any discipline no way out of formulating conclusions based on the evidence at hand. Since he regarded such conclusions really as 'a habit of the human mind rather than an expression of an order inherent in phenomena' (Breisach 1983: 210), Hume saw the refusal to draw at least some conclusions as a renunciation of the scholar's task. By the third quarter of the eighteenth century, among Hume's conscientious followers could be counted Adam Smith, the 'father of modern economics', who was to bring that empiricist influence to economic discourse. In so doing, Smith demonstrated the importance of an approach distinctly different from *a priori* investigation. A friend of Hume, Smith was educated in an empiricist environment and, not surprisingly, went on to entitle his *magnum opus* in economics *A Inquiry into the Nature and Causes of the Wealth of a Nation* (1776) (a sharp contrast to the Physiocratic *Tableau économique*). Like the empiricists, he reflected an unusually great reliance on observation and historical data in his inquiry into the economic 'nature and causes'.

Following in Hume's empirical footsteps, it is Smith and his fellow countryman Bentham who had the most profound impact on the methodology of modern economics (and on a few historians, such as Halévy, as well). Their faith in induction and empirical evidence provided the necessary 'facts' and steps for building and illustrating premises and theories; their philosophies of individualism, and especially Bentham's hedonism, brought the possibility of quantifying the catalysts of human economic activity. The study of human economic activity had become the product of both the science of things (material wealth) and the science of mind (ethics). The ideas of Smith and Bentham were to influence the two major succeeding divisions of thought in the economics discipline, the classical and the neoclassical schools. By the classical school, as represented by Ricardo, Malthus and Mill, economics, or political economy as it was called, was seen to be both a *science*, with respect to production and accumulation of wealth, and an *art*, with respect to its human involvement; political economy was referred to quite simply as a science by the neoclassical economists, a group which began to take shape at the beginning of the nineteenth century with von Thunen, Senior, Cournot and then expanded with the founders of marginalism, Walras and Jevons, to include Marshall near the end of that century.

The majority of economists from Smith on did not follow purely either a deductive or inductive process, although indeed examples can be found throughout the nineteenth century of economists like Ricardo who continued to favour strongly *a priori* reasoning, and others like Malthus who relied more on empirical fact. Marshall summed up the synthetic approach: 'It is the business of economics and of almost every other science to collect facts, to arrange and interpret them, and to draw inferences from them' (Marshall 1890: 24). Citing Schmoller's *Volkswirtschaft* in the same paragraph, Marshall quoted:

'Observation and description, definition and classification are the preparatory activities. But what we desire to reach thereby is a knowledge of the interdependence of economic phenomena . . . .

Induction and deduction are both needed for scientific thought as
the left and the right foot are both needed for walking.'
(Schmoller on *Volkswirtschaft* in Conrad's *Handwörterbuch*)

Then he continued, 'The methods required for this twofold work are
not peculiar to economics; they are the common property of all
sciences. . . . There is not any one method of investigation which can
properly be called the method of economics. . . ' (Marshall 1890: 24).

The role of observation and facts

Recognition of the need for a synthetic deductive–inductive logical
approach became especially acute as the nineteenth-century
economists moved away from the methodological debate about the
status of political economy as a science (moral or exact) and began to
discuss the role of observation and facts within economic science. As
empirical information took on greater importance, economic
scientists came to realize that the possibility of confronting theoretical conclusions to facts (i.e. a process of verifying) was extremely
difficult. This is already explicit in Mill (1950: 340) in the context of
discussing the appropriate methodology for a social science but more
clearly expressed by Jevons:

> The deductive science of Economics must be verified and rendered
> useful by the purely empirical science of Statistics. Theory must be
> invested with the reality and life of fact. But the difficulties of this
> union are immensely great. . . . But, before we attempt any investiga-
> tion of facts, we must have correct theoretical notions.
>
> (Jevons 1871: 22)

The philosophical individualism and hedonism of Smith and
Bentham were thus not the only catalysts to an interest in empirical
data on the part of economists of the nineteenth century. The
methodological posture of the German Historical School economists, as represented in their first generation by Knie and Litz and
in later generations by thinkers from Schmoller to Weber, also based
its analysis of human economic activity on empirical data.
Distinguishing itself from the British empiricists, however, the
Historical School adamantly attempted to recognize data as the
product of a historical context. Further the School's emphasis on the
assertion that each historical period has contributed something

distinct entailed the rejection of Benthamite individualism. A historical period's distinctiveness, it was believed, can be recognized only on the scale of the state and its society and understood only in the context of the period itself. A historical period's value or contribution can be judged only with reference to itself.

Any simple methodological emphasis on discrete facts, chronologically isolated, lacks, however, a systemizing theory; this lack left the German historicists susceptible to the ideas of contemporary and earlier philosophers' on historical continuity at least. From Leibniz' 'historical event as a "unique conjunction of forces"' to Hegel's 'progress of the Spirit and its spiritual entities', the states were to derive the Historical School's heavy composite of *a priori* premises. Leibniz' insistence 'on viewing the general and the individual as co-joined in every phenomenon' and his conviction that 'every historical phenomenon represented a complex and unique conjunction of forces' would prohibit the facile establishing of simple cause–effect relationships and by extension 'general laws' (Breisach 1983: 204). With Hegel, progress theory, persistently alive in the eighteenth century, received strong *a priori* philosophical expression in the 'Spirit', the study of whose dialectical process toward self-realization, the reason for historical change, should underlie all historical analysis. 'The history of the world is none other than the progress of the consciousness of Freedom; a progress whose development according to the necessity of its nature it is our business to investigate' (Hegel in Breisach 1983: 232).

For all adherents of the German Historical School, economists included, history was to be at the heart of every study. That history was to be 'scientific history' with its own methodological principle, von Ranke's *'wie es eigentlich gewesen'*. The School's 'scientific' posture meant primarily insisting on the rigorous examination of sources. It was to lead, on the one hand, to the smug rejection of earlier histories as inferior empirically and otherwise, and also to the naive assertion that 'history was no longer the servant of any other discipline'. This bravado also led, however, to scholars from most disciplines taking a new interest in history and to historians and economists discussing seriously the 'scientificity' of their task.[25]

In truth, any significant leap forward towards critical investigation in economics and history by the 'historicists', and most other nineteenth-century economists and historians, was overshadowed by *a priori* premises from decidedly beyond their disciplinary bounds.

First premises from theology led von Ranke to assert that conflict between states is not to be avoided, for 'over everything there lies the divine ordination of things which we cannot indeed directly prove, but which we can sense. . . .' (von Ranke 1973). Premises from Hegelian philosophy instilled in Marx a conviction in the *a priori* existence for history of laws governing the material conditions of human life. With this interpretation of a study as 'scientific', the comparison of theories to empirical data through verification was indeed to pose a problem. Thus, despite their serious methodological gropings, as they entered the twentieth century economics and history were both found to be lacking in the 'proper credentials' to be considered 'pure' sciences.

From Comte's positivism to the neo-positivism of the Vienna circle

Already in nineteenth-century continental Europe a different path to the 'scientifization' of economics and history had opened up with the positivism of Saint Simon and Comte. For Comte, positivism was the philosophy appropriate to a third and last stage, after a theological and a metaphysical stage, in the development of the collective mind of humanity. Ultimately, in the stage of positivism, Comte envisioned his philosophy of a positivist science applicable to all areas of human knowledge. In a positivist science all knowledge stems from observed facts and experiment, not from intuition or belief; experience permits the discovery of the laws governing phenomena, even social phenomena. In the positivist era one is able not only to understand, but also to predict collective progress.

Although among philosophers enough varieties of positivism ('evolutionary', the 'empiricritic' of Ernst Mach and Richard Avenarius, etc.) eventually sprang up to cause Comte's to be labelled social positivism, few historians were immediately excited by Comte's scheme and method. The reluctance of sympathetic scholars (Fustel de Coulanges, Langlois, Seignobos) seemed to stem from their sense that general laws of human activity, which might very well exist, could probably not be induced from available historical documentation, on which every statement must be totally based. There were, however, in time some notable historians who applied positivist 'scientific' techniques valiantly – for example, Buckle of England, Taine of France, and Adams of the United States. Initially, each of the positivist historians reflected a conviction in history as a science which, no doubt in part, sprang from a desire to make history available to a more fruitful methodology, an attitude well expressed by Monod in 1876:

> We have understood the danger of premature generalizations, of great *a priori* systems that claim to cover everything and explain everything. We have sensed that history should be the object of a slow methodological process of investigation in which one moves gradually from the particular to the general, from details to the whole; where all obscure points are successively illuminated in order to have the whole picture and to base general ideas, susceptible to proof and verification, upon groups of historical facts.
>
> (Monod in Gay and Wexler 1972: vol. 4, 105)

Some disillusionment is, however, detectable in those, such as Adams, who failed ultimately to see (verifiable) 'necessity' in the historical links they chose to explain.

Historians were indeed astute to have seen 'necessity' as an essentially problematic feature of the application of positivism to history. By the 1890s, with a stated aim of strengthening the respectability of many disciplines *vis-à-vis* science, nineteenth-century positivists had begun to drift further towards a method devoted to establishing necessary truth(s). Logical empiricism, or neo-positivism ensued as a method using the rigorous analytic languages of science, logic and mathematics to establish logical, necessary truths which were matched to empirical truths. The hypothetico-deductive method of the neo-positivists is empirical both by inspiration and reference: the axioms of its reasoning are identifiable with observable entities, and its conclusions claim to express a state of the empirical world. The philosophy of this school represented in the work of Ayer, Carnap, Hempel, Neurath, Reichenbach, Schlick, Waismann, among others, enjoyed a tremendous success, especially in the 1920s.

The legacy of Comte in its guise of neo-positivism advocated only one way to acquire knowledge about the world: via the method of empirical science. All neo-positivist theories are expressed as a single one or set of propositions or statements which are to be shown to be true or false with regard to experience and facts. Verification A, or the finding of empirical instance(s) in identity with the theoretical conclusion, early neo-positivists argued, is the only way to find out whether a statement is true or false. This concept was rapidly found by some to be too restrictive in problem solving, and among advocates of strong verification many began to rethink the whole notion of verification. The challenge ultimately elicited shades of earlier debates among philosophers about whether verification of a proposition is in fact possible at all.

Carnap (1936), a hard-core neo-positivist, reconsidered an earlier position he had taken, and suggested that one might speak of 'confirmation' rather than 'verification' of the law to find out whether a sentence is meaningful. In the same period, Ayer proposed a 'weak verifiability' criterion which requires that a statement be considered valid only if 'some experimental propositions can be deduced from it in conjunction with other premises [if need be] without being deduced from those other premises alone' (Ayer 1936, reprinted 1946: 39). Already a critic of logical positivism in the 1930s, Popper even more strongly later rejected all criteria for verification and proposed instead his own 'falsifiability' test as the empirical investigation criterion to judge a theory. According to Popper, a theory's conclusion can be empirically demonstrated only to be false, never the reverse. Theories are really accepted, therefore, because they have not been shown to be false and as such are better than earlier (now falsified) alternatives.

Popper is very interesting because he addressed the idea of scientific method in the social sciences. His stand on the judgement of theory as not being justified by observational evidence and his conception of regularity as non-deterministic are most relevent to economics and history. Many of his comments in these regards find an echo in the thesis of the present book. There are, however, some real difficulties in using Popper to try to draw parallels between the sciences and social sciences. His methodological 'conventions' concerning falsification, for example, that theories must be rejected if experimental evidence is found to their contrary, that experimentally 'refuted' theories must be definitively rejected, or that later theories must have more empirical content than earlier ones are not, it is argued, applicable to economics and history.

The real issue with any criteria of 'confirmability' or 'falsifiability' as with those of 'verifiability' is to establish the feasibility of making an assertion about the relationship of logical 'truth' to empirical 'truth' based on the comparison of the former with the latter through observation. What does it mean when one is not in obvious accord with the other? Should proposed logical conclusions give away when they do not concord with empirical evidence ? Does this seem to be called for more when tightly circumscribed circumstances are being examined or when one is certain that empirical evidence is 'true'? How is it possible to assert the 'truth' of empirical observation (a) when a cause may have many effects and the correlations within a subset of causes and effects are themselves changing, (b) when identification of all the causes and all effects through observation is not possible, and (c) when it is difficult to disentangle the various causes from the various effects? These are some of the difficulties which, it came to be recognized, had to be considered when establishing test criteria for situations encountered in economics and history. None the less, there were members of the Vienna neo-positivist circle who undauntedly advocated the application of their philosophy to economics and to history, the most articulate of whom were Nagel and Hempel: ('There is no difference [in attempting the impossible task of giving a "complete explanation of an individual event"] between history and the natural sciences: both can give an account of their subject-matter only in terms of general concepts, and history can "grasp the unique individuality" of its objects of study no more no less than can physics or chemistry' [Hempel 1942: 231–3]).

Some of the thornier general philosophical issues as well as the emphasis on the axiomatic and analytic approach of neo-positivism were addressed critically in philosophy in the 1950s and 1960s, especially by Quine (see his two dogma of empiricism), Kuhn, Feyerbend, and Lakatos.[26] More flexible concepts of research practice were proposed by 'paradigms' and their shifts, by the 'continuity of research programs' or in the assertion that theories ought not be judged once and for all at one point in time but evaluated in their time and over time. It cannot, however, be said that the discipline of economics has generally been responsive enough to these latest debates in philosophy to glean the best from them. In practice the discipline still seems instead to be vacillating between complete rejection or complete adoption of the neo-positivist model of a methodology.[27] The works, for example, of Hutchison and Robbins in the 1930s show the demarcation of empiricism from apriorism and reflect how economics was following, as it still continues to follow, the trend launched by positivists in the nineteenth century and extended by the neo-positivists in the twentieth century.

Neo-positivism and economics and history

The response by historians to neo-positivist doctrines and their revisions has been mixed, but for reasons different from those at work in economics. The responses seem to be of three kinds.[28] First of all, many historians simply turn their back on the 'science' of history. Indeed, the majority of historians never saw their discipline as proper grist for the neo-positivist mill. While this was in part fostered by neo-positivist philosophers themselves – such as Ayer, who considered history to be hopelessly outside the canons of neo-positivist thought – it was also due to the long legacy of historians and philosophers of history for whom 'scientifization' had no attraction.

The shutting-out of science in history has most notably taken the form of seeing history exclusively as an art. Historians pursuing this tactic have determined the historian's product to be an *objet d'art* designed to persuade of its insightful perception of the past by means of rhetoric[29] or by means of its transparency.[30]

The majority of twentieth-century historians, both before and after neo-positivism continue, however, to be held most strongly by the legacy of the reactions to positivist scientifization. Dilthey, Weber and even Collingwood have been and continue to be their mentors, with each of them receiving a new round of revivalist homages in works of practice or theory.[31] Dilthey's respect for the achievements of the sciences was coupled with a rejection of 'the attempts to see the world of human phenomena as an analogue of the world of atoms and mechanical forces and to separate strictly the subject and the object in all research. . . .' He felt

> Those historians would always fail who simply observed, counted, measured, found regularities, and consequently wished to formulate laws. Their method fit the natural world of necessity but not the human world of freedom and they could not grasp the complex process in which intentions, purposes, or ends shaped human actions.
>
> (Dilthey in Breisach 1983: 281)

As one practising historian put it:

> For today's generation of historians, the non-neutrality of 'facts' is a commonplace, a subjective perception of reality is a more important historical agent than objective reality, the fallacy of intended consequences, or the counter-factual conditional, all are the woof and warp of the training of most historians.[32]

These last historians, unlike their colleagues in the earlier noted groups, are, none the less not poised against the scientifization of history.

Their mentors acknowledged directly or indirectly the strides that history writing had taken by the time of their reflections. Even Collingwood, who adamantly asserted that 'historical thought, thought about rational activity, is free from the domination of natural science' (Collingwood 1946: 318), always took 'for granted that historians should continue to go about their business. . . by working from documents and other records' and 'actually insists that history is inferential not intuitive' (Atkinson 1978: 27). Thus, they too have not let the work of neo-positivist revisionists, particularly Kuhn, go completely unnoticed.

There is, however, yet a third group of historians which has responded to the reactions to neo-positivism by digging in its heels and persuading itself all the more strenuously of the absolute scientific nature of history. For these historians, 'facts' are taken for granted as neutral and can be gathered without *a priori* sets of research assumptions; for them the phenomena under study are regulated by laws. Cliometricians, such as Fogel, Engerman, Conrad, Meyers, North and Thomas, are the strongest historical collective to advocate 'scientific history' of this kind. Although antecedents much, much older than Hempel survive in their method,[33] their immediate inspiration derives from the conviction of the neo-positivists in general that science and history do not differ in subject matter nor method of reasoning. Not to deny their efforts to effect a methodological transformation of aspects of history,[34] their work has mostly been aimed at drawing conclusions from the statistical manipulation of some of the more easily quantifiable historical data (see Aydelotte *et al.* 1972). The most novel approach recently to rendering history a science was undertaken by Chandler (1984) in *The Science of History: A Cybernetic Approach*.[35] Supporting his approach with statements from Vico, Hempel and Nagel among others, Chandler sets out his method for using axioms, deductions, 'observations to test the consequences' and 'inductions which lead to generalizations (called also hypotheses, or laws)' to 'achieve a greater coherence in describing the influences and, within limits, completeness in trapping them' (Chandler 1984: 4, 5).

Economics also has its representatives in each of the first two groups, the rhetoricians such as McCloskey and the quasiscientific, such as Samuelson and Hahn. Despite the recognized difficulties in the application of neo-positivism, and particularly of Verification A, to the study of economics, assertions by its advocates seem to have won the discipline over. Economics in particular appears to be more committed than ever to proving it can attain the status of a scientific study, and to seeing neo-positivism as the route. In economics, warnings about the difficulty of verifying theories[36] which initially fell on deaf ears have simply vanished and never rematerialized. Neo-positivist methodology is clearly still very appealing to economics.

It is interesting to note that even within the groups of economists and historians which deny that their disciplines are sciences, a notion of verification draws attention. Particularly in the new neo-positivist context of statistical applications and its other contributions to the 'proper' techniques of empirical investigation, the notion of verification is undergoing change. As is clearly indicated in the following citations, the aim of econometrics does not stop at the confronting of theoretical conclusions with data (which in fact in this context mostly means fitting or refitting a model with data), but extends to the estimating of desired parameters and, most importantly, to the recommending of policies based on these calculations. Thus the results of Verification A have practical ramifications which impose an ever greater need for its viability as a fruitful methodological step in economics. The use of theoretical conclusions for prediction has been and remains the ultimate aim of econometric conclusions, reiterated from the 1940s until 1989 by three Nobel Prize winners:

Economic research, as the term is used here, implies the testing of hypotheses about economic behavior suggested by theory, a knowledge of our institutions, independent empirical studies, and other sources. Hypothesis testing is, however, only a first step. In the next stage, an attempt is made to derive quantitative estimates of the characteristics of acceptable hypotheses. In general, research is understood, in the present context, as a search for empirical validated generalizations about economic behaviour.

(Klein 1954: 3–4)

The ultimate goal of a positive science is the development of 'theory' or a 'hypothesis' that yields valid and meaningful (i.e. not truistic) predictions about phenomena not yet observed.

(Friedman 1953: 7)

La soumission aux données de l'expérience est la règle d'or qui
domine toute discipline scientifique. . . . Cette règle est la même pour
la science économique que pour les sciences physiques.

(Allais 1989: 3)[37]

The Comtian idea of a era which considers its branches of
knowledge positivist and therefore capable of revealing the eternal
constants underlying everything seems to have arrived to the
discipline of economics in neo-positivist guise and may well be in the
offing for history.

THE IMPLICATION OF SCIENTIFIZATION FOR
ECONOMICS AND HISTORY

The trend in scientifization is irreversible. What Iggers observed,
writing of history in 1979, is proving to be correct: 'Neither the
professionalization of history nor the search for scientific rigour was
going to be reversed in the twentieth century despite the philosophic
scepticism regarding the possibilities of a historical science' (Iggers
1979: 2). This statement is even more appropriate to economics. The
position taken here is that a scientifization of economics and history
is not to be lamented. A scientific method is essential for rigour and
coherence in any investigation, whether in economics, history or in
the natural sciences.

The real difficulty in the scientifization process lies in the
understanding of the verification step. Some form of verification is
not only desirable but necessary if theories in economics and history
are to be credible. The form employed presently is, however, that of
Verification A, and its role continues to be enhanced. Economics and
history can be 'scientific' without imitating the exact sciences in their
search for 'truth', and thus the form of verification of most use to
economists and historians may well not be the exact scientists'
Verification A. The widespread attitude that every declaration has to
be technical (which stems from equating the scientific method with
the mathematization and quantification of every aspect of the
problems under study), and the belief that symbols and data-numbers
can speak for themselves reveal in economics and history a lack of
necessary intellectual maturity and independence from the
sciences.[38]

The debates which have most concerned the economists and
historians of the post-war period have addressed verification, but

only indirectly. The differences of opinion have turned openly on the appropriate focus of the scholars' investigation, positions defended apparently according to subjective, ideological choices. The choices function as the principal catalyst to a vehement polarization of scholars into camps distinguishing themselves, though no longer fundamentally, by topic. It is actually their different methodological tools (statistical analysis, computer data collection, etc.), and hence their posture on verification which, more critically than subject matter, underlies their *parties prises*. In the next chapter it will be shown how bias and value judgements enter the abstraction, theory-building and verification steps of theorizing in economics and history, and thus how valuable is persuasion by consensus.

Chapter 2

The present purpose and role of verification in economics and history

It is assumed throughout this book that the purpose of economics and history is to understand better the world in so far as its parts are the subject of the particular discipline. To do so, economists and historians ask pragmatic, factual questions, such as 'what has happened?' and 'how has it happened?'. They also pose questions concerning causal relations: 'why has it happened?'. Some seek out answers as well to counterfactual and hypothetical questions, such as 'what would have happened if . . . ?' and 'what will happen?'. To answer any or all of these questions concerning phenomena of economic and historical interest, economists and historians first collect facts or observe the appropriate part of the world, advance a theoretical response and then proceed to check whether their explanation fits the facts. Difficulties for the scholar may lie not in what questions ought to be posed, but rather in the way the questions are answered through data and theory and in the way the empirical investigation is performed. These difficulties are the concern of this chapter.

If economics and history are to deal with actual social phenomena then their studies must at least at the start and at the conclusion have a connection to observation and facts.[1] In these disciplines, empirical evidence is thus considered crucial in establishing both a foundation for their theoretical models and the applicability of their conclusions. In principle, the role of evidence can also be very instrumental in the disciplines' aim for objectivity, by assisting in the elimination of subjective beliefs, value judgements or prejudices. To insure an informative relation between theory and evidence, economists and historians must be rigorous both in the selection of their evidence (*electio*) and in the construction of their theories. One way of instilling greater rigour would be to adopt the use of a verification process which could assess the strength of the theory (i.e. the ability of the theory to encompass the most content and the greatest number of variables, to explain the situation well and to explain it with the greatest simplicity) and also that of the data as evidence, by establishing an intermeshing relation between them.

In order to concentrate on specific past or present phenomena in the context of societal interactions, economists and historians attempt to distinguish within the world that part which pertains to their studies. They then isolate the part from the whole, by means of data or written documents, and referring to them as evidence encapsulate them in an abstraction. In the present chapter, it will be seen how empirical evidence, gathered over years or even centuries, comes to serve both disciplines, as the initial observational evidence on the basis of which the theory is conceived as well as the empirical evidence with which the conclusion is confronted. Difficulties encountered at the level of data compiling, theory building and verifying will be discussed. It will then be argued that bias and value judgements inevitably make their way into each methodological step.

Building a strong theory and obtaining, for both its first and last methodological steps, accurate, neutral data about the phenomena under study are not easy tasks, but ones which have to be undertaken with great care if verification is to play an important evaluative role. Verification, as presently employed in economics and cliometrics, is carried out from a foundation of data which is either not empirical or without evaluative potential. It is going to be argued that if facts (including circumstantial information) are selected as appropriate evidence without recognizing the limitations of the data to be representative, and certainly if the facts and their sources are not submitted to rigorous screening and scrutiny, Verification A is rendered pseudo-serious. Verification A, which uses data as the ultimate reference criterion for acceptance or rejection of a theory's conclusion, when applied in economics and cliometrics cannot actually function as a verifier; instead it serves as a convenient tool to justify theory. It should not be surprising, thus, to see different economists and cliometricians disagreeing fundamentally, although each advances assertions based on empirical evidence. Witness the many economic controversies, for example, between the monetarists and the Keynesians on the questions of whether governments can affect unemployment or whether there is a relationship between unemployment and inflation, or the cliometricians' debate on the relative agricultural efficiency of farms worked by slaves and free labourers (Fogel 1982: 99ff.).

As to verification as an evaluative process, the economist and historian, unlike the philosopher,[2] are primarily concerned with its being able to establish theoretical conclusions as having empirical relevance at least under specific circumstances, although rarefied by premises such as *ut in pluribus* and *ceteris paribus*. When presented with data which appear to be counter to their conclusions, economists and historians may rightly feel that their theories have neither been necessarily 'refuted', nor proved to be in need of revision. Oftimes, however, they can be so stubborn in adhering to a conclusion they reveal that it functions less as the necessary suite to the immediate model than to the extensive layers of theoretical premises. This does not mean that economists and historians are not responsive to an exercise of 'verification', which they want to see as assessing their conclusions. Again, this should be no small wonder, for as presently conceived Verification A functions virtually as a step of theory justification.

The philosophy of neo-positivism inspired economists and historians, among scholars of other disciplines, to adopt Verification A, a methodological step of checking theoretical conclusions against empirical data. In fact, since scholars often build their models on value-laden premises (such as the positive value of government fiscal intervention for the welfare of a nation, and the greater efficiency of slave over free labour), when they proceed to verify their conclusions the empirical data chosen most often conform to the subjective premises. Indeed, this is often the kind of data which cannot help but reinforce the conclusions being checked. This pseudo-verification is at the heart of the discussion in this chapter. In the process of Verification A, as understood if used by quantitative economists and historians, doubt can fall only on the theoretical conclusion and, by extension, on the theory, never on the data taken as evidence; 'as scientists we must always remember that, when theory and fact come into conflict, it is theory, not fact, that must give way' (Lipsey 1963: 533).

In the guise of a check on theoretical conclusions, this kind of verification reinforces existing schools of ideas rather than advancing knowledge. Ironically, it is the very adherence to the positions of schools, laden with partiality and bias (inevitable, due both to the discipline's particular focus and the unavoidable involvement of the scholar), that renders the theoretical conclusions of economists and historians vulnerable to rejection. As part of the effort to win acceptance of their theories, economists and historians may vigorously employ Verification A, which appears to impart an objective scientificity to their work. They are at the same time actually resorting to consensus as the way of defending their arguments, for given the type of verification used its results cannot serve as grounds for rejecting or accepting a theoretical conclusion. Not really a checking procedure at all in economics and history, Verification A none the less functions as the step by which scholars reassure themselves and their audience of the impartiality of their theoretical conclusions, and possibly even assert their discovery of a 'law'.

THE PRESENT ROLE OF EVIDENCE, THEORY AND VERIFICATION

Presently the role for verification is determined primarily by the use of statistical correlations in theories as if the correlations signify causal relations. In most economic theories, correlations among variables are established, according to empirical data, and used to build theoretical models. Although the nature of historical facts is often too qualitative and amorphous to allow statistics to be employed, among historians, cliometricians at least also put great stock in a method of analysis through variables. As shall be seen, even in specific theories where correlations among variables can be easily established and well supported by data it still remains doubtful whether such correlations can detect cause and effect relations between phenomena, not to mention disentangle causes from effects. Doubt stems from various reasons, among which is the fact that causality acting on phenomena of interest to economics and history is not deterministic. In the context of causality of a non-deterministic nature, a quantitative model is unable to encapsulate the causal relations of economic and historical phenomena, and a process of Verification A, which consists in establishing through tests the consistent one-to-one correspondence between the theory's conclusions and actual facts, is both impossible to carry out and meaningless in presumed results.

What kinds of facts are used by economists and historians, and what role does verification play when generalizations pertaining to those facts are asserted ? How do economists and historians theorize and verify?

Facts as evidence

To study economic and historical phenomena, data cannot be created as in the experimental sciences.[3] An economic outcome or historical event is specific to a particular time and place; it can neither be replayed nor recreated. It has often been repeated that the only facts available for both disciplines are recorded data. In economics the data are mostly about prices and quantities in various productions, about factors of production, stocks of goods, financial, monetary and physical assets, sales and purchases, etc. In history there are all kinds of documents about past events specific to particular times and places: letters, written descriptions, analyses, accounts, testimonies, edifices, pictures, etc.

It is undeniable that, in toto, there is no dearth of data for economists and historians to use; new technologies and ideas are constantly improving the gathering, compiling, storing, manipulating and increasing of information about past events. Despite its now overwhelming amount, it remains that the best available quality and quantity of information still gives an incomplete picture of what actually took place. It is simply not feasible to record with total accuracy every detail in every place all the time. In addition, what is recorded is abstract; it is averages or aggregate measurements in the case of economics and, in the case of history, accounts specifically structured in form or content as records, paintings, stories, buildings, poems or depictions. Thus, whatever form and quantity of information happen to be available constitute the only sources of evidence economists and historians have on which to build their empirical premises and conceive their theories about phenomena.

As mentioned earlier, the attention of economic and historical scholars is attracted to information about distinctive or similar characteristics of events or outcomes. Similar combinations of like characteristics of economic and historical events are seen to reoccur or repeat in different circumstances; these give rise to recognizable patterns of activity, such as economic depressions and expansions, wars and peace, the rise and fall of political powers, etc. It is in large part the perceived existence of such patterns which leads economists and historians to search for causation and to come up with generalizations about phenomena of economic and historical interest. Some important questions concern this search: given the available facts, can causes be identified? and, more importantly, are the causes at work in the events which seem to be part of a pattern

always the same? In both economics and history the available information is used to formulate many alternative theories about single
phenomena such as consumption or investment behaviour, monetary
transmission, revolution, war, slavery, religious conflict, etc.

Example and theory

An example of a perceived pattern in economics, the business cycle,
has been chosen to illustrate how, from the same pool of
observational data, alternative theories, built from different premises
and yielding different economic policy implications, are constructed
and how each one could comply to the test of Verification A.
Observed fluctuations in economic variables, such as production,
employment, prices, etc., led in the first and second quarters of the
twentieth century to a flourishing interest in theories of business (or
trade) cycles. A recession phase came to be identified as a period in
which prices, interest rates, wages, investments and capacity
utilization all tend, relatively, to be low, while unemployment, stocks
of goods, and idle money are high. A prosperity phase was also
identified in which the reverse occurs. The classic economic crisis
came to be defined as a sharp downturn in the overall level of
production, and thus as an event dramatically marking the change
from prosperity phase to recession phase.

Interest in describing and explaining the business cycle was
fostered greatly by economists taking special note that, following the
Industrial Revolution and particularly during the rapid expansion of
the nineteenth century, the industrialized economies had undergone
numerous economic crises.[4]

While the list of business cycle theories has now grown too long to
be cited in full, the few examples that follow should suffice to
illustrate how competing theoreticians of one group each advance
the claim of explaining the cause and the effects in the cycle, and
perhaps its crisis points as well. All the theoreticians can be divided
into two groups. There are the economists, such as Slutsky (1937),
Frisch (1933) and Lundberg (1937), who believe that economic
changes are due to *exogenous*, random shocks. Frisch, for example,
argued that the market economy is frequently subject to erratic
shocks, in the guise of crop failures or technological innovations,
which momentarily disturb its smooth functioning but that its
internal market mechanism will bring it back to a stable level (to an

'average equilibrium path'). Using differential equations, Frisch designed a mathematical model in which erratic impulses create a dumping effect and make the level of economic activity converge towards an equilibrium path; such impulses, erratic but reoccurring, will perpetuate a cyclic movement.

A host of other economists in a second group explain the business cycle in terms of *endogenous* economic causes. The causes of its fluctuations are described in their alternative theories as being the driving forces of either demand or supply, monetary factors or government policies. In each of these theories, dramatic fluctuations are seen to result from dramatically increasing discrepancies (or lags) between selected major economic variables. The economic forces which tend to narrow the gap between these variables are thought to be the triggers of the cyclic movement. Examples of this second kind of explanation can be found in the following theories:

Wicksell (1898) explained the cyclic movement in terms of discrepancies between the real rate of return (the rate of return on investment in industry) and the monetary rate of interest (the bank rate). When economic activity is slow and money is idle banks offer low rates of interest. When bank rates lag behind the rate of return on real investment then the gap between the two rates (in favour of the rate of return on investment) encourages investment. As the economy expands, however, the demand for money or credit starts to rise, and the money rate begins to catch up with the real rate of return. As these two rates get closer, the profit margin from investment decreases and investments get discouraged; the situation is then reversed. To simplify the picture, for Wicksell it can be said that it is the ongoing conflicting interaction between the banking system and industry which causes fluctuation.

Hawtrey (1928) explained business cycles in terms of the degree of confidence in the economy and the availability of credit. Expansion and contraction of credit depend on the prevailing amounts of economic optimism and pessimism. As credit increases, so do prices (this is inflation), which in turn raises interest rates. The increase in bank rates continues to the point where investment begins to be discouraged. Then a deflation phase takes over. For Hawtrey, fluctuations are thus monetary phenomena due to a succession of inflationary and deflationary effects; the interaction of cyclic importance is between the banks and the public at large.

Kalecki (1936) suggested that it is the delay between the decision for and the realization of investment which is the major cause of cyclic movement. When the demand for goods and services starts to increase it usually takes time first to plan and arrange for financing, then to order new equipment and to install new plants. Increased demand sends signals into the market upon which producers start to act (not knowing whether any other firms are acting in the same way). Often, however, when the new equipment becomes operational the market finds itself in overproduction and decisions to invest start to slow down. This in turn has an effect on production at some later period. For Kalecki, cyclic fluctuations are caused by changes in the demand for new equipment.

Hayek (1932–3) and *Robertson* (1933) argued that increases and decreases in government spending create inflationary and deflationary effects. Due to these effects, investment comes to be diverted from sectors producing capital goods to sectors producing consumption goods and vice-versa, and consequently cyclic economic fluctuations occur.

Mitchell (1923) attempted to show that discrepancies between receipts and cost of production are the cause of economic fluctuation. When profits are high firms increase their investment; as their production capacity increases, so does the demand for factors of production, which in turn increases the cost of production. This increase diminishes the rate of profit, which in turn slows investment and eases the demand for factors of production. Mitchell's explanation of cyclic economic fluctuation rests entirely on supply-side changes.

Goodwin (1967) analysed economic cyclic fluctuation in terms of class struggle. In a recession, when unemployment is high, workers accept relatively low wages. As an economy tends towards recovery and labour becomes scarce workers can organize and make effective demands for higher wages, using strikes if necessary. When higher wages are awarded profits start to decrease, as does investment. Thus, for Goodwin, cyclic fluctuations are explained in terms of the distribution of income between social classes.

Here the choice of theories explaining the business cycle by endogenous causes was made on the basis of the ease of explaining them, but a number of other discrepancies, such as investment/saving, effective demand/purchasing power, expected rate of return/market rate of return, etc., have also been suggested as decisive (Haberler 1937). In the last decade interest in business cycles has notably revived (for example, Kydland and Prescott 1982, Lucas 1987). Lucas claims, in fact, that the improvements in mathematics have led present explanations to surpass earlier theories, particularly as they render dynamic the analysis which before was static (Lucas 1987: 2). Despite an undeniable advance in the use of mathematics in their analysis, the newest theories are, however, not really any different from the earlier ones. The fundamental issues remain the same, and none of the new theories is any more immune than earlier ones to the problems which are addressed in this chapter.

In the case of each theory, the idea was to construct a model in which changes in any two economic variables, believed to be major ones, are deemed to be the initial driving causes for economic fluctuations and according to which changes a cyclic movement can be established. This does not mean that variables other than the initial ones are not thought to be present in the movement being described. They are taken as lagging behind and are, therefore, not considered causes, but effects. Theoretically, there is no difficulty in building a mathematical model using difference and/or differential equations to generate a cyclic pattern on the basis of lags between two major variables. As Burns pointed out in criticizing Hicks's theory of the trade cycle (1950): 'Any competent logician, especially if he has the command of mathematics, can select a set of simplified conditions and deduce a cyclical path from what he has assumed' (Burns 1952: 2).

A theorist's choice of one set of variables over another has absolutely nothing to do with the use of a scientific method or the degree of a model's mathematical sophistication. No one set is more appropriate for model building than another. Assuming, as has been maintained from the start, that economic theories are all conceived fundamentally according to a similar 'scientific' method, then one cannot judge any one theory, except for logical consistency, by assessing its procedural steps. How does this translate into the specific problem of economic fluctuation here? If a 'scientific' method has been applied the theorizing steps might well be similar in the following way:

After some empirical investigation, one would assert the *hypothesis*:

The principal cause of economic fluctuation is the changing discrepancy between the variables x_i and x_j chosen from among the set of variables X.

Then one would employ at least the following basic *premises*:

Fluctuation is defined as changes in the level of economic activity.
(Definition)

There is fluctuation in the economy.
(An empirical premise)

Economic fluctuations are caused and those causes can be known.
(An epistemological premise)

Agents who cause changes in xi and xj do so out of self-interest.
(A premise from behavioural psychology)

i is different from j.
(Specification of the model)

xi and xj can be quantified.
(An epistemological premise)

When xi differs from xj fluctuation ensues.
(A theoretical postulate)

xi and xj are interactive features of the economy.
(An empirical premise)

The set of variables X includes other features of the economy,
(An empirical premise)

and they may function as secondary causes.
(A theoretical postulate)

xi and xj are considered *ceteris paribus*.[5]
(Specification of the model)

Next, one would construct a *model*:

The logical relationship between xi and xj is constructed, according to all the premises including the mathematical specifications, to reflect the hypothesis. The model is thus the internally consistent demonstration that when variables xi and xj are correlated their theoretically specified relationship exhibits theoretical fluctuations.

Finally, one would assert the *theoretical conclusion*:

A comparison of the theoretical fluctuations the modelled variables describe with those of the economy at large is such that the pattern of fluctuation of the former precedes a similar pattern produced by the economy at large. From this correspondence, causality is inferred and an explanation is provided to assert that the principle cause of economic fluctuation is indeed the changing discrepancy between the variables xi and xj.

All of the above models are made to depict, with greater or lesser complications, the perceived cyclical movement. All have similar general hypotheses and premises; all use models in theory building; all come to their conclusions based on the same strength of argument by inference. If internal coherence is lacking within the model then it is immediately subject to rejection. If, however, the logic of the theory cannot be faulted on what basis can one then decide which one from the multitude of theories is a good one?

Before discussing the role of verification as the criterion for choosing a correct theory it can already be said that value judgements of scholars are incorporated both in the choice of initial variables as well as in the specifications of the model. The chosen examples of business cycle theories readily reveal that ideological schools of thought are reflected in the theories. For example, depending on whether economists believe that the market economy is inherently stable (Frisch, Hayek, Robertson, Mitchell) or inherently unstable (Hawtrey, Harrod, Kalecki), the specifications or restrictions of their theories' models will be designed to contain dampening, cyclic or explosive effects, according to which market forces play either a stabilizing or destabilizing role. The choice of particular leading variables as the driving force may also imply that something can be and is to be done, if fluctuations are to be reduced. For example, if government intervention is built in as the initial cause of the perturbations then the policy implication of the theory is to advocate the reduction of its intervention. If the bank plays the initial role in the perturbations then some control on the banking system will be suggested. If a Marxist class struggle is seen to be the cause then the theorist will argue that the exploitation of workers, apparent during prosperity, is devastating during economic slumps, and since capitalists will always use unemployment to break workers' unions and lower workers' product share workers should be better unionized. Another theorist might blame workers and unions for economic fluctuation and suggest ways the free market might be used to reduce the power of unions. It is important to realize that such opinions and presuppositions often make their impact felt even before the theory has been formulated.

Now what about the argument that only empirical evidence will tell which theory is right? This touches most particularly on the work of econometricians and cliometicians, who take empirical evidence to be the sole criterion for judging theories. It is thus important to ask what it is that econometricians and cliometricians do and how do they perform Verification A.

As Marschak, one of the influential founders of the study of econometrics and a founding member of the Cowles Commission (as an affiliate of the Econometric Society) established in 1932, stated it, 'Quantitative economics study has a threefold basis: it is necessary to formulate economic hypotheses, to collect appropriate data, and to confront hypotheses with data . . .' (Marschak 1950: 1). 'Formulating hypotheses' means here the specifying of models in mathematical terms (see Johnston 1963). Marschak also wrote:

In its Annual Report for 1944 and for subsequent years, the [Cowles] Commission stressed the importance of adopting statistical methods to the peculiarities of the data and objectives of economic research. The economist's objectives are similar to those of an engineer but his [the economist's] data are like those of a meteorologist. The economist is often required to estimate the effects of a given (intended or expected) change in the 'economic structure,' i.e., in the very mechanism that produces his data. None of these changes can he produce beforehand, as in a laboratory experiment; and since some of the changes envisaged have never happened before, the economist often has to estimate the result of change that he has never observed.

The economist can do this if his past observations suffice to estimate the relevant structural constants prevailing before the change. Having estimated the past structure the economist can estimate the effects of varying it. He can thus help to choose those variations of structure that would produce – from a given point of view – the most desirable results. That is, he can advise on policies (of a government or a firm).

(Marschak 1950: 2)

The aim of the early econometrics of Marschak and the Cowles Commissioners consisted in finding correlations among variables. Their study was not to be pursued naively, and the difficulties with economic data and phenomena were recognized and discussed from the start. Marschak's statement reflects some of the observations already made here: that laboratory experiments cannot be conducted to test economic situations, that economists deal mainly with counterfactual questions and that the questions seeking answers are posed 'from a given point of view' and a result is identified as 'desirable' according to value judgements. The quotation also reflects the concern of economists in implementing policies based on the results of economic theories.

It seems, however, that with time the aim of the econometrics of Marschak and the Cowles Commission has slowly shifted ground. Econometrics tends at present to be understood, by such representative econometricians as Granger, Theil, Zellner, Hendry, Judge, Griffiths, Hill, Lutkepohl and Lee, as a search for causal explanation. '... the primary objective of econometric modelling is to provide an "explanation" for actual economic behaviour (which can include descriptive and predictive aims as well)' (Hendry 1985: 29).[6] What this means is that econometrics is becoming ever more ambitious and claiming a much greater significance for its theories. 'Econometrics is concerned with the empirical determination of economic laws' (Theil 1971: 1). Policy recommendations based on laws can hardly be ignored.

Verification

In principle, verification is a process of comparing the conclusion with the facts. If the way of staging a comparison is to fit the model with data and to perform statistical tests then, technically speaking, the process of verifying is that of Verification A. A theoretical conclusion is seen to predict 'future' events, which, because they have in fact already occurred, provide the data against which comparison of the conclusion can be made.

In the context of such theories, can empirical evidence perform a check of the conclusion?[7] As are many theoretical econometricians, Johnston is well aware that 'No economic data ever give an exact fit to simple relations of this kind since linear or other simple forms are only an approximation to possibly complex but unknown forms and also since only a small subset of all possible explanatory variables can usually be included in any specification' (Johnston 1963: 6). Yet, as Johnston notes, econometricians have come up with a way of dealing with the problems they perceive: 'These factors require the specification of a stochastic error or disturbance term in each relation other than identities' (Johnston 1963: 6). Hence, it is argued that the difficulties can be surmounted, and Verification A can be performed with 'new' data. Indeed, the data chosen to verify the particular model will probably fit it quite well.[8] As will be seen, the 'success' of

Verification A is in part what fosters its use in applied econometrics and cliometrics.

Business cycle theories will continue to serve as a good example here. Economic activity is frequently subject to fluctuations. Slumps and peaks designate the low and high levels of activity of the economy. In macroeconomic dynamics, variables such as employment, production, investment, savings, capital, labour, profits, prices, interest rates, wages, income, taxes, etc. are all correlated to each other; during different phases of the cycle they change relatively to one another. During an economic expansion phase it is most likely that changes in wages mean changes in profits, that changes in the cost of production mean changes in prices, that changes in investment decisions mean changes in investment realizations, that changes in the money rate of interest mean changes in the rate of return, that new investment means new savings, that changes in government revenue mean changes in government spending (note that an increase in revenue has not prevented governments from cumulating deficit after deficit in the last two decades). As the economy reaches its peak and starts to slide towards a recession the demand for goods and factors slows down and the mentioned discrepancies between the key economic variables narrow. It seems, therefore, that a time series of past data of any set of economic variables describing a discrepancy will reveal a correlation among those variables, which, if the hypotheses about the business cycle are modelled properly, will exhibit a rise and fall.

Now, if one is to consider the actual business cycle and decide, for example, which one of the theories best describes the phenomena, one might find that all the above theories are possible candidates. These theories describe general movement, and their variables encapsulate aggregate or average magnitudes. Even though a slow-down in economy activity may indeed mean a decrease in the quantity of production, employment, demand, investments, prices, rates of interest, etc., an economist can only speculate as what causes what. The only thing the data and model can show is the correlations that appear to exist between certain variables. They would not be able to reveal which variable's change is the *principal cause* of the cycle and which changes it effects.

From a macrodynamic viewpoint economic fluctuations are continuous movement resulting from the cumulative changes taking place in an economy in different sectors, industries, regions, etc. For example, at one point in time, an increase (for whatever reason) in the rate of interest may have an impact on some sectors of the economy and not on others; firms with large cash flow, for instance, will not be affected by such a change as much as those sectors with a shortage of liquidity. Simultaneously, certain sectors or firms may be experiencing labour disputes; others may be having difficulties selling their products; for still others the demand for their products may have just started picking up. Due to differing expectations, some firms may decide to increase their capacity of production, while others reduce theirs. In addition, these changes may be occurring in one part of the country, while in another part different events are happening at the same time. Governments also play a role as they adjust their policies to respond to social or political pressures exerted themselves in response to unexpected changes, as, for example, new strains in the foreign market.

It is the on-going, cumulative effect of all these changes and their chain reactions and feedbacks which generate economic fluctuations. It is thus possible, within a wide range, for an advocate of a particular theory to emphasize one aspect of these changes and come up with a plausible explanation of the cycle phenomenon, when in fact advocates of other theories can do the same. It is furthermore quite possible either that many, or even all, of the variables, active in the ways described by rival theories, are at work or that some descriptions might reflect what is happening some of the time, and others what occurs at other times. It will be argued in Chapters 3 and 4 that the dynamics of the changes in question – ones which cause a series of other changes which, in turn, cause more changes, etc. – are directly linked to actions and reactions within the social fabric and are, therefore, not deterministic. The plurality of possible explanations for the business cycle is thus simply one instance of a non-deterministic circumstance about which neither a model nor data can determine which variable is its cause, which its effect.

It has already been noted that, in the case of economics and history, the neutrality and coherence of mathematics and statistics or the use of scientific method (which are not faulted) cannot exclude value judgements from entering into theories from the start. They are not in themselves sufficient to guarantee the neutrality or objectivity of economists and historians. It seems that in the absence of theoretical laws supported by phenomenological laws they are not in themselves sufficient to guarantee the neutrality or objectivity of economists and historians. The reasons are several:

1 A theory's evidence, its data, is facts in the form of measured approximations which may well be as theory-laden as the theory they try to support;
2 Choice of variables and specifications are either *ad hoc* or a result of value judgement;
3 The verification procedure is a circular process, since one abstraction or theory (the theory) is checked by another abstraction or theory (the data).

Having considered the data and the choice of variables, of concern now is the verification procedure. Is there such a process as the comparison of a conclusion with facts which could counter biases? Formerly in cases in history and even in applied economics (for example, earlier theories of business cycles), although the conclusion, explaining a particular situation or a generalization from it, ensued from observation, verification in the sense of 'subjecting the assertion to test' was rarely performed. Disagreements were often settled by the method of appealing to an authority in the field – for example, 'Keynes said so', 'Marx confirmed that', 'according to Pirenne it can be affirmed'. The strategy was one way of answering the question of who could play the role of verifier of a conclusion: could it, should it, be the scholar proposing the conclusion, or must it be another, such as the community of scholars at large? At issue, however, was really what would constitute a procedure of verification at all. There is a distinction to be made here, of course, between Verification A, as performed in econometrics and cliometrics, and Verification B, as practised by a few economists and by a large number of historians.

Verification A was meant to be a test of whether the theoretical conclusions match the phenomena theoretically explained. Thus, theoretical fluctuations of the business cycle should be shown to match phenomenological fluctuations. Yet, just to start, the choice of variables highly determines the choice of the time series data, upon the extension of which the verification step must depend. Verification A is really a process of affirmation rather than of verification. Econometric theorists, even more than applied econometricians, reveal an awareness of these difficulties. Leamer is direct in asserting 'Economists have inherited from the physical sciences the myth that scientific inference is objective, and free of personal prejudice. This is utter nonsense' (Leamer 1983: 36).

The illustration of the present understanding of facts, theory and verification demonstrates that difficulties abound in the abstracting, theory building and testing of economic and historical phenomena. Attention will now be turned specifically to those difficulties.

PROBLEMS IN THIS CONCEPTION OF THE ROLE

In many disciplines abstracting, theory building and testing have become more and more engaged in by scholars working in teams, either in separate teams devoted each to one aspect of theorizing or working together as one team on all three parts.[9] It is, however, as always, still only a few individuals who are responsible for leading the way for each area. The majority adopt the ideas of the few and 'model their clay' around them. This section addresses issues concerning the way in which leading-edge theories come to be. It should not, however, go unmentioned that while followers of another's ideas may share the other's concept they may well not all have the very same abstract vision, neither of the phenomena concerned nor of the way their abstractions correspond to the phenomena themselves.

In his example of population study, in the *Grundrisse*, Marx seems to have captured the crucial steps in theorizing:

> ... if I were to begin with the population, this would be a chaotic conception [*Vorstellung*] of the whole, and I would then, by means of further determination, move analytically towards even more simple concepts [*Begriff*], from the imagined concrete towards ever thinner abstractions until I had arrived at the simplest determinations. From there the journey would have to be retraced until I had finally arrived at the population again, but this time not as the chaotic conception of a whole, but as a rich totality of many determinations and relations. The former is the path historically followed by economics at the time of its origins .... The latter is obviously the scientifically correct method. The concrete is concrete because it is the concentration of many determinations, hence unity of the diverse. It appears in the process of thinking, therefore, as a process of concentration, as a result, not as a point of departure, even though it is the point of departure in reality and hence also the point of departure for observation [*Anschauung*] and conception. Along the first path the full conception was

evaporated to yield an abstract determination; along the second, the abstract determinations lead towards a reproduction of the concrete by way of thought.

(Marx 1857–8 in Hausman 1984: 164)

Abstracting, theory building and verifying form what Marx called the 'process of thinking as a process of concentration'. The process consists, for Marx, in beginning from reality as a 'chaotic conception' and moving analytically to an 'imagined concrete' from which a total picture composed of many simple determinations can be derived. His point of departure is observation; his point of arrival, the 'reproduction of the *concrete by way of thought*'.[10] Marx does not allude here to any difficulties one might encounter in the 'process of concentration', but they lurk not far out of sight.

Difficulties in abstracting from a complex world

What are the problems faced by economists and historians in transforming their perceptions of the world into a record of the facts abstracted? The greatest difficulties arise from the restrictive focus of the abstraction activity.[11] Restriction is an inevitable necessity, given the complexity of the world and human biological limitations for receiving impressions, encapsulating information and holding and translating impressions and information into records. Impressions of the world, obtained directly through the five senses and further through information collected, are dictated by one's contact with it. Such contact takes place within the limits of specific time(s) and place(s).

Economists and historians try to make their contact with the real world as broad as possible and hence try to combat inherent limitations to their experience of it. Such attempts usually incorporate some form of mediated contact between the principal scholar and the real world, such as extensive collections of data for vast spans of time or space, of which whole scholars can make use (even as they may contribute to it), or the use of a team of individuals (of which the scholar is only one), involved simultaneously in collecting empirical data. These attempts can be quite successful in combating the limitations of the lone scholar. They may, however, lead to other difficulties in further steps of the formulation – for example, the impossibility of creating a theory for many generations/lifetimes as data collection is still ongoing, or the need for restrictive specifications of the 'kind' of data under investigation in order that all the scholars involved observe the same kinds of pieces of reality.

The necessarily restricted focus of the abstraction also poses a different collection of difficulties. Scholars find themselves not only limited by their inability to be everywhere at once and to experience the events of all time, but also by their incapability to process into an abstraction all the information available to them. This second limitation means that most scholars are in the process of learning about only one small part of the evolving real world at a time. Thus, despite the fact that research may yield new information, that information forms but a tiny, new part of an already existing large body of abstraction the scholar holds in his memory. The restricted rate and scope of human information absorption/abstraction means that most of the body of abstraction each of us carries around inside is not new, and the new portion can have only a limited impact on the old corpus of abstractions.

What does it mean to say that new information will change only a little bit of the whole mental picture of a scholar? A relatively static conception of the world, held in memory, is what dictates our theorizing process and is the framework into which the new information must fit. It is this static conception which permits or determines the focus of the abstraction.[12] In the rational human being only those parts of the static abstraction which can tolerate an influx of new information are permitted to be shaken. This implies a choice in the focus of research which is neither random nor involuntary.

It is perhaps not so easy to see that intellectual choice is imposed by the scholar's mental limitations, for it seems simply to be the outcome of the profession, the specialty within the profession and personal prejudices or bias. These are, however, all manifestations of choices dictated by the capability of human beings in general and individuals in particular to deal with new information. Each of these conditions, and all of them together, impose a restrictive focus on a scholar's abstraction. If their imposing force is not recognized at all the scholar is in a sense at their mercy, and little of the static mental construct of the world will be vulnerable to change from new information. If, however, the scholar is aware of these limitations, at least in part, they can be appreciated as such and may even be stretched to extend the capacity of the static conception to absorb more and more new information.

Difficulties in theorizing

While human memory is limited, fallible, and forgetful, human imagination, on the other hand, can expand beyond almost any limit. The mind can indulge in all kinds of hypotheses, dreams, fantasies and unreal abstractions. Its impressions of the world are comprised of both the reception and the creation of images. Some images are objective; most contain subjective elements. The interpretation of every impression is affected by feelings, sensations and moods. No matter how removed they try to be, economists and historians can thus not totally escape some subjective considerations in their analytical work.

The human mind processes all the knowledge that has been acquired through direct and indirect observation and encapsulated in an abstraction. Through logical reasoning, the abstractions yield laws or theory-bound conclusions. Laws distinguish themselves from theory-bound conclusions not in their being necessarily any different in conception. Each may begin in hypothetical limbo, as an idea newly conceived or adopted from earlier results; some earlier results inevitably turn up as premises. The mental formulation of each is organized logically. In neither case are all the elements questioned; components may be taken for granted.

Laws and theory-bound conclusions are distinguished, however, in the degree to which each is connected to the theory from which it derives. The meaning of a law is considered to be theory independent, referent only to empirical observation and operationally definable, while that of a theory-bound conclusion reflects the premises on which it was built and the coherence and cohesion of its arguments. While both may take the form of a single statement, the theory-bound conclusion implies a network of statements. For disciplines like economics and history, whose body of knowledge is far more dependent on theory-bound conclusions than on pure empirical laws, the problems of communicating ideas are unavoidable. The limitations inherent in conveying the results of the thinking process in a language that others can grasp (symbols, graphs, words, images, etc.) are thus significant.

No matter how articulate and adept, a scholar will always have some degree of difficulty in expressing thoughts not only (a) simply in attaching words to ideas to his or her personal satisfaction, but also (b) in finding terms which will be understood as desired by the receiving audience.[13] The difficulty of communicating fosters the need for and security in either the statement of the theory's conclusion as a purely empirical law or the strong adherence to a group whose language is common and predefined. Statements in the form of empirical laws seem to eliminate the confusion of com- munication, for their meaning is ostensibly immediately intelligible through empirical information and they are as independent of the 'language'-limiting stages of their formulation as they are independent of theory. Adherence to a group, however, seems also to eliminate confusion in communicating, by reinforcing through jargon, conventions and group consensus the sense that all is understood by all, permitting many things to be considered 'taken for granted' and avoiding much struggling with concepts. As shall be discussed further, many economists and some historians seem to be striving to be understood both through law and group acceptance of theory-bound conclusions.

The problems in communication are compounded when scholars attempt to combine experiential information and deductive components into theories. Economists and historians both use inductive and deductive reasoning and information in the process of conceiving theories of human behaviour and societal interaction. The application of both processes presents itself because the scholars' subjects are part of the observable world, and yet at the same time the serious appeal to imaginative constructs can further theoretical expression. Coordinating the two processes requires, however, the creation of 'correspondence rules' between the theoretical terms and ideas and the observed data. The well-established link ought to render general or idealized statements inducible from empirical data and testable statements deducible from theory.

Quantitative economists and historians appear to believe that the need for correspondence rules has been fulfilled with the use of mathematics and models. 'Let x be a consumer . . .', 'let y be a slave woman . . .' may persuade some that the evocations of 'consumer' and 'slave woman' have been connected to certain observed activities. It is disputable, however, whether, for example, economic 'rationality' is adequate shorthand for an important deductive concept.

Thus, given the human limitations of storing information and interpreting perceptions, the capability of the imagination to expand on information for theories, and disjunctures of communication between the two, distortions may well enter into theory building about the complex world and in turn become embedded in a theory's conclusion. When one studies human behaviour and societal interaction one unavoidably mixes objective and subjective elements into both inductive and deductive reasoning. Thus, in addition to the other difficulties, no matter how the theory is established it cannot escape some degree of value judgement. Relying on both empirical laws and a common language, scholars thus form their groups to reinforce each other's convictions; that reinforcement goes a long way in assuring the survival of a theory or law agreed upon at the time. The stronger the conventions and the convictions, the less any form of conclusion is exposed to questioning, and the more mechanistic the support for it. The use of the phrase, 'objective, scientific theories' would appear to be unwarranted in economics and history.[14]

The difficulties in conceiving verification

Being the passage which suffers the greatest number of limitations, the link between theory building and verifying is perhaps the weakest in the whole theorizing process. It is also the least analysed of the steps. Apparently, when others criticize one's theoretical conclusion it is much easier to fall back on the excuse of the inadequacy of the data than it is to question that version of one's theory presented for verification.

The most rigorous conception of verification implies that all components of an asserted theory must be reducible to verification. To make the theory available for the scrutiny of its every detail, devices, conceptual and technical simplifications or complications, are introduced. These transformations, which add to the limitations inherent in the earlier steps, now distort further the results of each step of the whole theorizing process into something which cannot possibly bear resemblance to the way the phenomena under study were initially presented.

Does verification do justice to abstraction? At this theorizing step it may come to be revealed that, in fact, the verification process has in a sense 'predictated' the scope of the abstraction. The scholar may have chosen for abstraction only that portion of the real world which is tangible and quantifiable, as it was deemed from the start to be the only part easily subject to verification.

Does verification do justice to theory? It is becoming more and more fashionable to rely on mathematical models as well as the widespread technical, statistical methods of empirical testing (econometrics in economics, cliometrics in history) to study phenomena of economic and historical interest. The greatest difficulty faced by a scholar concerned with verification is to find specifications which satisfy both the theoretical conception of the phenomena under study and the convenient formulation the theory should take for the use of standard statistical techniques[15] to be possible. The difficulty of conceiving an adequate theory of a phenomenon which at the same time satisfies the formulation needed for statistical manipulation is often unnoticed.[16] It seems the scholar determines a formulation of the theory convenient for statistical manipulation *a priori* (by approximations, linearizations, analogues, etc.), even if the theoretical conception will be weakened. Or, as is becoming more and more the practice, the scholar shortcuts the human contribution to the theorizing process and relies more on the computer to point out an appropriate technical model. The practice consists in suggesting one or more possible models and in letting the outcome of statistical methods (on the basis of, for example, the R2, T test, F test, DW test) determine the best model, and hence the 'best' explanation of the phenomenon. Not to mention the neglect of theory, the mechanical problems inherent in such statistical procedures reveal that between certain variables a correlation indistinguishably good or bad can be the outcome.[17]

There are other more general consequences of this understanding of the step from theory to verification. First, to conceive of the process in this way is to see as paramount an adjustment of one's perception of the world as well as one's theoretical conception to compliance with standard statistical techniques. Second, to put the theory at the mercy of statistical techniques[18] in the conviction that they, and they alone, can suggest the 'best' model is to restrict human creativity in theory conception.[19]

Does it make sense to permit economic and historical theories to abandon the role of explaining all parts of human activity which cannot be reduced to tests accessible to anyone? Does not this interpretation of verification restrict the scope of the theories and require them to ignore the fact that most of their events are unreproducible, hence unreproduced by a test, and neither reducible to the singular for observation nor extrapolatable to the plural for generalization? Is not the real purpose of the exercise for economists and historians lost?

Verification is seen to be the checking or testing of one's theory against reality. Its methods, therefore, must be devised to carry out that purpose. Can the verification procedure as presently understood by economists and historians, in fact, actually function as a test? Obviously it is easy to point out that the laboratory of scientifically controlled experiment is unavailable. Verification is dependent for 'new' evidence, therefore, on other less controlled conditions and sources. To wait for time to pass is considered too inefficient a way to reaccumulate pertinent data.[20] The past is the only easily accessible source of a reality against which to compare the theory. Confirmation in the past is, however, no guarantee that what one concludes is applicable in the present or future, a fact which is crucial to economics.[21]

Does verification establish that a match is possible between theory and reality? Some scholars clearly consider pertinent 'reality' to be statistical data. Although it is clearly a restrictive notion, for an economist or historian who is also an astute statistician it might in fact prove a functional one. In the early days of econometrics the researcher alone compiled the data, using them first to inspire and construct theories and then to verify them. Today, however, when the data available to an economist or historian are the product of an army of statisticians aided by computers, the scholar has an abundance of information provided, as it were, on a silver platter. In the rush to incorporate them, however, strict criteria of their use are not established, and the essential questions about how they have been prepared go unasked.[22]

To note the least, statistical data, if not one's own, are someone else's abstraction; much more important, they are always theory-laden.[23] Verification based on statistics becomes, therefore, redundant. The match it establishes between theory and data is artificial when extended to the real world. Difficulties do not diminish, however, if by 'reality' one means the not-so-easily-quantifiable dynamics of human interactions, which at one point in time led to the conception of the theory. Through verification one can never really return to the complexity of the phenomena observed to prove or disprove their match with the theory; theories per force simplify those phenomena. Also, the dynamic world against which one verifies is no longer the same as that one which motivated the theory in the first place; hence it cannot prove or disprove the validity of the theory.

The task given to verification by positivists is perhaps far greater than it can perform, certainly in the disciplines of economics and history. It is acknowledged that scholars have to make a choice in the aspects of reality they study and have to simplify their explanations. They cannot, however, at the same time expect their theories to surpass the limitations of their premises and abstractions.

Ironically, because the limitations are often forgotten and the need to have one's theories accepted persists, while carrying out the procedure of Verification A economists and historians are really resorting to consensus as the means to validate their theories.

IMPLICATION OF THESE LIMITATIONS

Verification and confidence

The need to obtain consensus,[24] wide acceptance of one's theory, has led not only to an unbalanced emphasis on verification, but also to the divorce of the verification procedure from the process of learning and discovery. Verification, or checking, in acquiring an independent status of its own has assumed three complementary roles. It confirms for the theoretician the solidity of the theory. It provides for others a test of the theory. Lastly, it may even permit the theoretical conclusion to be affirmed universally as a law.

The first role for verification epitomizes the shift in the importance of verification as an epistemologically significant step. Its function is no longer to extend the scholar's road of discovery, but instead to confirm that its end has been reached. When the scholar checks the correlation between theoretical claims and chosen categories and quantities of empirical evidence at best it is done with the intention of using the most appropriate method for judging whether or not the theory is a 'good' representation of reality. Once the theory is verified to a scholar's satisfaction the scholar feels, therefore, that it can be strongly espoused, in the confidence that it is a solid, justified perception of reality. The scholar is thus reassured by this role of verification that the theory is indeed well-founded and ready for acceptance.

As part of its first role, verification also serves to detach the scholar from the theory. It helps the theory's designer be persuaded that in abstracting and theorizing one can act as an 'impartial observer' of the world. The scholar can thereby be reassured first of the accessibility of a theory to others, and hence of its acceptance by others. More than that, through verifying the scholar may become reassured of the 'absolute' objectivity of the theory. In considering only the first role verification now assumes, it is already clear that, though its significance to the theoretician has shifted drastically, its importance has certainly not waned.

The second role of verification, that of providing a testing procedure, underlines again its importance in serving as the 'objective' stamp of approval to a subjective theory. If a theory is verifiable its claim to objectivity is generally deemed merited, and this because through the process of verification the theory is considered accessible to anyone who would choose to test it. A test then seems generally to be a highly desired component of a research method, because when a theory can be tested its elements become accessible to general scrutiny. The process of verification may force a theory to be open to scrutiny and perhaps to be able to stand up to the ensuing criticism of its elements or conclusions. Verification can thus offer the test, in fear of which the scholar controls his flights of fancy, but also in honour of which the critics accept the 'seriousness' of a theory and the gravity with which it ought to be considered for acceptance or adoption. The third role of verification is that it may serve as the vehicle by which a theory might receive a universal stamp of approval for the ultimate objectivity of its formulation: it might serve to affirm the discovery of a law. The accessibility to scrutiny, in principle, which verification can afford for any available theory emphasizes the potential universality of that theory's conclusions. For those conclusions that can withstand unrelenting comparison to empirical information, verification offers the process by which that comparison can be effected. It also provides the ground for concluding 'scientifically' that when so consistent and tight a correlation exists a fundamental, universally true statement has been made. Along the model of the physical sciences, then, verification in economics and history is deemed a possible (and essential) means for determining whether or not a conclusion is in fact a law.

In the context of Verification A, the discovery of a law is deemed the ultimate goal. Although laws are more restricted than theories in their application and less abstract, in that if testable they must refer to concrete entities, in the model of the physical sciences their discovery is highly valued. Testable through comparison to observation alone, a law is a statement deemed to be independent of

its theory, unlike most other conclusions, which are, for their understanding, theory-bound. Theories which function as explanations of
laws may be revised or replaced, but the laws themselves remain a
constantly accurate way of understanding the empirical world. Thus
as the verification process holds out the hope of a contribution as
potentially permanent as a law, and the fame connected with such a
contribution, its use becomes more and more widespread.[25]

The ability of verification to fulfil in economics and history the
three roles attributed to it seems widely accepted. As has been seen, the
importance of the process of verification has grown to the point of
devouring the territory of the other components of the theorizing process. The increasing reliance on testing has corrupted and diminished
both the role of theory and of observing. Verification, as it is conceived and conducted presently in economics and history, suffers from a
number of drawbacks, for which evidence can be found in every step
leading to the conception of a theory and beyond to its interpretation.

Partiality and bias

Econometrics and cliometrics, part of the disciplines of economics or
history, share in the objective of their respective whole study: each
aims to offer a better understanding of the world.[26] Reinforcement
for the effort may derive from a sense of participating in the
accumulation of knowledge. On the one hand, one might see oneself
at the point of directly advancing knowledge; on the other hand, one's
contributions might be the 'raw material' readied for 'cutting edge'
analysis by others. The real difficulty for every economist and
historian to achieve the individual goal, of fostering for all a greater
understanding of the world, lies, however, in the lack of a single
method by which each can convince others of what constitutes 'a
better understanding of the world'.

To meet the objective it is usually not enough for the economist
or the historian simply to advance a theory. Presentation of a theory
may indeed be sufficient to convince *some* individuals of its worth, i.e.
of its valuable correlation to reality. For the most part, however,
more than that is required to persuade people of a theory's ability to
explain reality and to have it widely accepted.[27] A lack of immediate
universal appeal of their theories is disconcertingly obvious to most
historians and economists. While they are keenly sensitive to
lukewarm acceptance or flat-out rejection, it is not always clear how

aware they are, however, of the reasons for the reserve of their audience. As has already been discussed, most theories, at least initially, are curtailed from a rapid, broad appeal by the limiting aspects of the theorizing process itself. These limitations are further compounded by those of the individual scholar. Any process of abstraction limits its empirical source. Subjects for abstraction are per force restricted by the focus of the respective discipline, and are then even more tightly defined by the scholar's interest and expertise. A theory is in effect predetermined to be a conception from an abstraction of a part, and this in turn yields a specific and partial analysis of the world.

A feature which certainly limits the easy adoption of a theory by others is the scholar's involvement.[28] The scholar, as part of the observed world, cannot when analysing it stand outside, totally objectively detached. Perception of the world is thus determined, to at least some degree, by a scholar's place in it. Both the scholar's position in that part of the world specifically observed and individual value judgements and personal convictions about the world in general (about human beings, their behaviour, their potential, etc.) are highly influential to a scholar's perception. The initial abstraction of the world and the fundamental hypothesis on which the theoretical model is built, and in turn the model itself, are determined to some degree by individual bias.

It is indeed scholars' partiality and bias in economic and historical theories which often renders their conclusions vulnerable to rejection, to a lack of general recognition, or at least to an unenthusiastic embrace. Aware or not of the reasons for a reaction, economists and historians grope for a way to convince others of the validity of their theoretical conclusions. A teleological component, while it may still be a feature of a theory, no longer serves to unify scholars as a criterion for assent; instead the methodological step of verification is today deemed the most promising way to obtain assent. As has been noted, however, due to the ineffective way of verifying, through Verification A the economist and the historian, including the econometrician and cliometrician, today must further affirm the general significance of their theories by another means; the means favoured is consensus.[29] Consensus appears satisfactory, for if enough individuals have been persuaded of the correlation between the theoretical conclusion provided and a designated body of data and accept the theory, they form a sufficient, if temporary, loyal body of supporters to sustain the ideas, at least until a new alternative is advanced.

Verification and consensus

Thus, despite the partiality and internal bias of the theory, the scholar is all too ready and willing to render the theory advanced accessible in order to obtain consensus support for it. Obtaining consensus is rendered possible if the theory is available for examination and for comparison. There is general agreement that the only kind of theory which is available for examination and comparison is one which is susceptible to empirical verification.[30] Empirical verification, in the form of Verification A, is deemed so important that its procedures for making a check of the theoretical conclusion available to all have, in fact, had the effect of moulding the types of theories that can be developed. Quantifying devices, conceptual and technical simplifications or complications are introduced into theories in such a way that, as noted earlier, a theory itself is brought to the point of serving the verification process.

The emphasis on letting consensus determine the importance or worth of a theoretical contribution does not yet, fortunately, mean that all economists and historians believe that there is or ever will be only one correct theory. Every theory, accepted or not, represents one individual's perception of part of the world. Discrepancies between the theories of different individuals may be due to the process of abstraction itself and to the individual's choices. A more important reason, however, for discrepancies between theories may be the strictures imposed on a theory in order to make it available for acceptance, i.e. for verification. It is quite possible that scholars who might be very much kindred spirits may find themselves in a relatively insignificant but extremely divisive disagreement with one another over the minutest pieces of a verification routine.

The roles attributed to verification – confirming, testing and affirming – appear to limit it to the part of the theorizing process which tests the theoretical conclusion. But verification also has implications on how a theory is initially conceived and how it is subsequently readied for subjection to empirical tests. If, as asserted, economics and history are indeed concerned with the actual world then their theories must both derive from the world and serve to reflect it.

REALISM

The concluding suggestion above might seem to indicate that the thesis developed in this volume is about realism. In a sense it is. If realism is defined as the conviction that theories refer to 'real' or 'existing' entities then a realist's perspective is significant to this discussion in at least two major respects.

A realist's conception of the world is essential for the disciplines of economics and history to exist. It has been stated frequently already that the purpose of the studies of economics and history is 'to obtain a better understanding of the world'. The statement clearly implies the existence of a world to understand. That world is one which not only exists, but exists independent of the separate scholars who study it. Only thus can all who share in its study come individually and collectively to a better understanding of it.

In the second place, a realist's conception is essential both for expectations or predictions to play a part in theory building and for Verification A to be performed. Both prediction and a process of verification which depends on the observable replication of facts in order for a theory's conclusion to pass the test, require a conception of economic and social events as forming a continuous course which is ordered, regular and independent of the particular observer. To consider model building and predicting as serious enterprises is an indication that the model is conceived as a reference to the 'real' within the theory. For prediction and verification, thus, the world of the particular economist and historian must exist such that it can be observed (and even predicted to exist) as such for other economists and historians. The premise must be that independent 'reality' exists, well-behaved and accessible.

As will be discussed in the next chapter, economic and historical phenomena are, however, complex and do not exhibit regular behaviour. Theorizing about these phenomena is, therefore, difficult. To some degree the epistemological postures of reductionism, instrumentalism, operationalism and rationalism have proved and can continue to prove useful in the two disciplines. The interpretations of the conclusions from such approaches must, however, be recognized to be at best approximations and, as is more likely, speculations.

Reductionism is one attempt to acknowledge both the role of empirical information in theory building and the difficulty of establishing a link between that role and the theory's arguments. Economists and historians who recognize that their theories do not refer exclusively to observables and do not conclude with statements subjectable to Verification A might find some use in reductionism.

Its technique is to employ short-hand conventions to reduce the content of the theory to observation statements. The observation statements themselves in being general enough to embrace new observations without needing adjustment must prove to allow prediction. Reductionism provides at best approximations, for its conventions cannot be explicit enough to lead to exclusions; it is speculative, for it maintains that its conventions do represent something, and a large range of observable entities at that.

Instrumentalism and operationalism are both approaches which are seen to be avoiding contributing to the discussion of correspondence rules. They assume that theories are not abstractions in the sense of interpretations which encapsulate a picture of the world, but rather that they are tools, calculating devices or instruments for organizing and relating observations. Although observations are the catalyst to the form the instrument or operation takes, no link between them and the components of the theory, let alone its conclusion, needs to be posited. If one takes an instrumentalist or operationalist position as far as prediction is concerned, one makes 'no claims to the literal truth of any of the theorizing that accompanies or surrounds the generalizations; one is free to use models which are given a purely "as if" interpretation, and are justified solely on the basis of the prediction-rule they generate' (Coddington in Marr and Raj 1983: 74). In principle, instrumentalist and operationalist theories are message without medium.

In fact, instrumentalism and operationalism have led some to assume that functional predictions can emerge from the 'black box' of formal calculus. The epistemological approach of instrumentalism and operationalism is, however, recognized by others to be inadequate to perform the explanatory functions demanded of its models. The arbitrary choice and stipulation by convenience of theoretical variables will yield fictitious conclusions, nothing more. In making no connective link to an empirical source their theories can neither describe nor explain, and on what grounds can they still claim to predict any actual event? Thus, in addition to approximations working as points of departure, in instrumentalism and operationalism speculations are paraded as solutions.

Rationalism is the approach which focuses on the 'ideal' or logical relationship of the theoretical components. It holds that 'rational' principles determine the conception, construction and evaluation of theories. It countenances belief in the entities its theories describe and explain, while acknowledging that the theories themselves can be evaluated only according to rational values of logical cohesion, plausibility, simplicity, etc. The strength of rationalism in certain disciplines is the response of some to the investigation of unobservable aspects of their subject. While rationalism can claim to be very subject specific, it can only appeal to logic to reject criticisms of speculation.

How might economists and historians take advantage of the variety of epistemological approaches without abandoning the realism essential to their disciplines? First, it might be recognized that realism is already at the foundation of all the other epistemological approaches. For reductionists it underlies the short-hand conventions and the conviction in the predictability of individuals as part of the group. Although instrumentalists and operationalists must deny any vital dependence on 'real' entities, it is their existence alone, however, which gives meaning (or lack of meaning) to their exercise and most especially to their results. Rationalism is often the epistemological approach of pragmatic anti-realists, scholars who see little gain in confining their subject matter and their theoretical constructs to what can be empirically observed. Economic and historical rationalists may well be those to believe in the 'reality' of that essential, wide spectrum of entities, observable and unobservable, which those of other epistemological persuasions are wont to ignore.

Next, economists and historians might benefit from suggested philosophical 'middle' postures, particularly as they confront the issue of causality. Philosophy of science is groping for such solutions to explain impasses in science between theoretical constructs and directly and indirectly observable reality. In a middle position between strict realists (who presuppose 'reality' before claiming to understand it) and anti-realists, Hacking, for example, advocates establishing the reality of particular entities on the basis of practice and by appeal to 'home truths' or low-level generalities about their causal properties (Hacking 1983: 265). Hacking denies that if a theory is true then the theoretical terms of the theory denote entities which are causally responsible for the observed phenomena. Observation and manipulation alone provide the best evidence for what is real; 'home truths' are the best guide to cause-and-effect explanations.

Morrison (1989) has for her part objected to Hacking's quite pragmatic approach to evidence for the 'real' as well as to the 'epistemological burden' he places on 'home truths'. She, too, none the less, advocates a middle ground, placing renewed emphasis on the epistemological steps of 'knowing what we are doing and that we are doing it'. Her observations could well be adopted as significant caveats for economics and history: crucial theoretical commitments are involved in the development and adoption of theoretical techniques, from surveys to statistics; techniques can be used in contexts where there are no firmly held beliefs about the entities being manipulated; manipulation (observation, test, etc.) may not always be possible, yet in such instances scepticism about the particular entities may be unwarranted. Morrison's objections to Hacking's role for 'home truths' may, however, be more valid for the sciences than for economics and history. Although their set may be small, as shall be seen in Chapter 4, it is quite possible that a few 'truths' which 'remain robust under theory change' and aloof from 'the kinds of complex theoretical frameworks that are normally taken to be definite of a theory' would, in economics and history, open the door wide for discussion and inspiration among the present factions in the disciplines.[31] Does, however, the foundational realist posture of an economist or an historian mean in the end that prediction and Verification A are possible? As will be seen in the next two chapters, the realist's conviction that a world 'exists' beyond the individual scholar, while it may permit one to be persuaded that events can be predicted and assessments of them tested, does not oblige such a belief. Belief in the possibility of prediction and empirical counter-tests depends not on the mere independent 'existence' of the world, but on the existence of a particular kind of world. The world in which prediction and Verification A can be exercised requires a regularity of activity in all its parts, human and material, and an uninvolved observer to appreciate that regularity. The conditions for prediction and Verification A may present themselves in the material world of which human beings are not a part, however they are significantly lacking from the world of the economist and the historian.

Chapter 3

Societal dynamics

COMMON CHARACTERISTICS

Verification A is indeed being presently employed in economics and history, on the assumption, methodologically that it is just as appropriate to them as to the sciences, and philosophically that it is just as implementable. In order to evaluate this adoption of verification, it is important to examine economics and history for any aspects of those studies which are unlike the sciences and which might be significant in the light of verification. The four duals which economics and history have in common in their study are just such important aspects:

1 The reseacher is an observer of the world but is also intimately a part of it;
2 Conceptually a distinction is made between man–nature and man–man relations;
3 The human subject is both passively a spectator and absorber of information and also actively an actor and creator of ideas and decisions;
4 The human activity of concern is made up of the individual and the social group interacting and influencing one another reciprocally.

None of these duals is inherent in the studies of the exact sciences. This means that none of the implications of the duals will have been faced by exact scientists.

In order to examine just how ill-suited Verification A might be for economics and history it would be appropriate to establish in what respect their four duals are pertinent to the discussion of verification. Once the effect of the four duals on theory building in economics and history is recognized, the validity of their adoption of Verification A from the sciences ought to be immediately questioned. The duals are an inherent part of every aspect of economics and history; they pertain in their methodologies and their philosophical premises. If so, what must then be the implications of having the duals of observer and participant, human and non-human, individual passivity and activity, and individual and group reciprocal action as features of a discipline's study? For separate reasons, as will presently be discussed, the duals undermine three conditions which some disciplines consider essential to their ability to study their subject matter: a detached objectivity of the investigator, the ability to observe all conditions which are theoretically potential causes of an outcome, and the ability to set up a control observation environment. A far subtler implication of the duals, however, is their role in the analysis of the regular occurrence of events under scrutiny in economics and history. As has been noted since Aristotle, regularity of phenomena allows the easiest access to understanding them; yet within these duals lie the seeds of indecipherable irregularity.

THE FOUR DUALS

Economists and historians as observer and observed

Observers of human activity by vocation, both economists and historians are, none the less, themselves connected to human activity, and thus in part identify with it. As the creators of their studies, the economist and historian alike function as human beings in a double role, the human investigators of human subjects like themselves.[1] It is this dual character of human involvement within the discipline which makes economics and history, in a sense, allied in their difference from the non-human sciences such as physics. Physics, although also undertaken by humans, is concerned only with the study of matter, not identifiable particularly as human. Over time investigators of the physical world have come to recognize the degree to which its subject matter, from gravity to sub-atomic particles, can, and in fact ought to be, studied as abstracted from all human connection.

The majority of economists and an increasing number of historians like, however, to believe that the observer of the human world can be equally detached from the object of investigation. Is it possible for economists and historians to be completely detached from their study? As the discussion in Chapter 2 about bias, consensus and confidence demonstrated, total detachment of the researching economist or historian is impossible. Even a conscious distance from the research subject, while a desirable goal, is extremely difficult to acquire. The unavoidable involvement of the economist and historian in the study will be further evident in the following discussion of societal dynamics.

The research distinction between man–nature and man–man relations

In terms of their subject matter and the research posture of economists and historians to that subject matter, both economics and history share much affinity and distinguish themselves thereby in some respects from the exact sciences. Both disciplines conceptualize their scope as embracing two inseparable kinds of human relations. One, a 'man–nature' relation, is seen to be the relation between human beings and the non-human components of the world; the material aspect of the world is emphasized, albeit in its connection with human beings. The other, a 'man–man' relation, is that of human beings dealing with each other; the interaction of people is of primary importance.

The dual represents in economics and history an interwoven dynamic complex of material relations and human behaviour. The man–nature relation is focused on the material world and portrayed as the human struggle in that world (a) for survival and (b) for improvement or progress through material transformations with given resources, endowment and technology. Material relations comprise thus both the realm of tools and materials in producing both necessary and accessory goods and services and the situation of individuals or the group within a natural environment. The man–man relationship has to do with social organization and the role of individuals in the group.

If the two pairs of relations can be separated from one another, in theory at least, then the first can be conceived technically (e.g. in the keeping track, by calculations or accounts, of human contact with and manipulation of the physical world). The human behaviour of the man–man relationship focuses, however, on the decisions and actions of individuals or classes as consumers, managers, warriors, worshippers, leaders and labourers. More behavioural and ethical, it entails value judgements and other subjective as well as objective human considerations. It cannot simply be treated by mechanistic theory. The difference of methodological approach for each pair has much to do with the fact that they do not both comply to the same dynamic forces.

Economics and history do distinguish themselves from physics, which is concerned only with nature and by extension the interaction of man with it, in that they do not consider just nature with man but also the relations of human beings among themselves. Undeniably, however, in both disciplines, the study of the relation of human beings to the material parts of their world figures prominently, analysed, for example, in the study of the production and consumption of goods or the accumulation of wealth in economics, and pioneering voyages of explorers or animal husbandry practices through the centuries in history. In both disciplines as well, the material aspects of such man–nature relations are mostly considered to be quantifiable. Unlike the case of the pure sciences, however, the research aspects of economics and history which can be quantified are definitely limited. Not only do human beings not relate to their material surroundings in a purely mechanical, calculable way, but even less can the economically and historically important interactions purely among human beings be considered effectively quantifiable. A non-quantitative conceptualization of the man–man relation, how individuals act and react among themselves, is an especially crucial component of the disciplines of economics and history.

While scholars in both disciplines have dealt with its material aspect, as well as with the behaviour of people individually or as a group, and would probably acknowledge that the two are intricately interwoven, in each discipline scholars seem also to have felt obliged to weight the importance of research towards one of the two relations, man–nature or man–man. Often the chosen emphasis is part of the larger discussion which finds scholars already divided in defining the boundaries of the discipline,[2] its significant subject matter,[3] and what the role of theory should be in its methodology.[4] Presently, in each discipline, though more strongly in economics than in history, there are those who believe that their study should be limited to calculable relations (as it were) and they thus simplify human behaviour to a set of rule-bound actions and then apply a rigorous method of analysis borrowed from the exact sciences, logic and mathematics.[5] Simultaneously at work in each discipline are others who believe that the prime concern of their study should be human relations and that human behaviour cannot be formalized in the same way as physical relations in the sciences.[6] It was with some nineteenth-century economists and historians that these postures began to be reflected in the context of the duals man–nature and man–man. This is already evident in the economic works of Malthus, Mill, Walras and Jevons and in the historical writings of Montesquieu, Bodin, Reclus and Febvre.

Is it, in fact, possible to separate the man–nature and the man–man relationships? Examples from economics might lead one to believe it so. Authors like Malthus, Mill and Senior referred to economics as a moral science, and favoured in their conception of 'political economy' the man–man relation. In the marginalist economics of Walras (1954: 79) and others economists are to be concerned with the man–nature relationship and to leave everything else to non-economists. Still other economists, represented most strongly by J. B. Clark, while willing to consider the man–man relationship, do not conceive the approach to it to be appropriately any different from that to the man–nature relationship and propose to demonstrate that the same scientific laws which govern the production of wealth also govern its distribution.

In history, distinction between the two relations is most frequently not emphasized as sharply as it is in economics, due perhaps to two reasons, noted by Barnes: historians' 'dominating interest in episodes' and their impression that a sharp division implies materialistic doctrines of determinism.[7] None the less, it is possible to find historians who made the distinction. Historians such as Carlyle and Froude, eloquent Romanticists, rejected accounts which did not focus on the man–man relationship. In deterministic history, however, the man–nature relationship dominates and denies a role for history in the description or analysis of the man–man half of the dual. Other historians, such as L. Stone (1977), while acknowledging the man–man relationship, have considered important components of its analysis to be no different in method from that of the man–nature relationship. Following the leadership of Buckle, some historians have even proposed to demonstrate that an approach which includes laws is equally appropriate to human beings in interaction with one another as it is to events in nature.[8]

The individual as active and passive[9]

A third dual significant in economics and history is that of the two roles of the individual, passive spectator and absorber of information and actor and creator of ideas and decisions. On the one hand, individuals are seen as passive, in the sense that they are influenced by their impressions of past events, as recorded in their memory, and present events, to which they respond without manifest action. On the other hand, they are seen as active, since they originate their own thoughts and choices, make decisions and within their capabilities act on those decisions.

Although not disassociable, the two parts of the dual, passive spectator/active actor, are contrastingly distinct. The receiving of 'raw' information through the senses is engaged in passively by the individual. Rousseau believed that individuals are born 'good' with innate ideas, and that it is society which corrupts them. In this study it is advanced instead that individuals begin unimprinted, as it were virgin, with respect to sense information. For the fetus, baby, then child, the senses develop and yield to the individual all kinds of information. Much information, both from observation and experience, is collected and stored by the individual. It teaches what at a specific time and place is 'good' and 'bad', what to do, and what not to do.

Individually, persons have both the ability passively to receive and process information from and about the world, as well as the faculty actively to think, to reason. They are considered to function actively when they turn the passively received information to their own ends in the form of ideas, propositions, and feelings and take decisions which lead them to act. The decision is the hidden outcome of the active process; the realization of the decision, the action, is the perceptible outcome of the process. While the dynamic process of perceiving–reasoning–deciding is internal to the individual and not observable, the expression of an individual's decision is external and observable in its manifest form. An individual's decision becomes materialized as an activity within the group. The acts of consuming, fighting, building, worshipping, hoarding or donating, or running for election are all manifestations of an individual's decisions.

Both the capacity to absorb through the senses observations and experiences which constitute an individual's vision of the world *and* the capability to reason per force as a separate entity constitute human individuality and the uniqueness of human acts. Human beings are both limited and different in their capacity of absorption and their capability of reasoning (for whatever reason). Thus they have different experiences and different ways of idealizing or conceptualizing in the mind. It is these differences which allow individuals to express themselves distinctly in thoughts and actions, which are thus labelled 'original' or 'creative'. It is also these differences which make it difficult for an observer to tell which decision will be made, as well as when and how this decision will take form.

It seems that the duality of individual as passive and active has not been given much attention in the work of theoretical economists and historians and yet its implications for both disciplines are numerous. If the dual is acknowledged individuals, which are the subjects of economics or history, can be considered to be neither predictable machines nor identical components of a collective entity. An understanding of the human decision-making process is also extremely important in the analysis of the chain of causation leading to events of economic and historical significance. Questions, such as what motivated an individual to act in one way or another?, what is the cause of a human action?, pertinent to both economists and historians, reflect that some understanding of human psychology is essential to both disciplines.

Economists and historians need not divert their attention fully to psychology but do need to understand its investigations in the light of their discipline. As psychologists are well aware, tackling a passive/active duality in which much that transpires is unobservable poses research difficulties. From the point of view of behavioural analysis, puzzling out how a decision is reached is far more problematic than deciphering the carrying out of a decision. The source of actions is problematically abstract, subjective and non-observable to other individuals. Only the actions themselves are noticeable to an observer and therefore subject to analysis.

The reluctance with which many psychologists connect an individual's unobservable decision to an observable action has found its counterpart in economics and history. Once a mental choice has been selected by an individual, a decision taken, then any ensuing action might appear to be the simple result of a mechanical carrying to term of what has been decided. For a number of reasons, however, few decisions are so directly realized in action. Most decisions undergo revision after revision, such that many decisions are not followed by actions at all, and individuals are often at a loss to link an action to the specific decision which led them to act. Hence, empirical scholars in many fields avoid drawing conclusions about the way in which individuals' actions are the reflections of their decisions.

In an exemplary way, the economist Shackle in his *Imagination and the Nature of Choice* (1979) acknowledged and confronted these difficulties in the context of economics, considering it an essential part of his discipline to have an understanding of the relationship between the taking of an individual decision and its fulfilment. Shackle focused on three stages in which choices and a decision originate in the mind of an individual. The individual gets impressions or information from the environment, or 'field' as Shackle calls the collection of both past and present events. Then there transpires a process whereby the mind sorts, transforms and classifies its impressions and information into 'arrangement–possibilities of abstract typical constant elements' – Shackle's 'scheme'.

Finally, there is the creative participation of the individual. To make decisions, individuals create in their minds, according to their own experience and ability, a series of alternative imagined choices – Shackle's 'imagined deemed possible'. Even though in their thinking individuals take into consideration their impressions of past and presently available information, it remains the case that a choice is something which originates in their minds and is not presented to them as given or derived by deterministic rules external to their mental processes. Thus the 'psychological dynamics' of Shackle, with its steps from impression to transformation to creativeness within the mind, clearly considers the passive and active duality within individuals.

A number of historians have lamented the lack of interest and emphasis placed on discussions of the mind of the individual by their colleagues. While

. . . it should be obvious that it is impossible for a historian to understand the behaviour patterns of men in the past without a knowledge of the general psychology of human behavior. . . . Nothing is more apparent in conventional historical writing, particularly in biographical writing, than the pathetic lack of a knowledge of technical psychology on the part of even many of the most talented literary biographers, with the result that all too often grotesquely superficial explanations are offered for personal motives and actions.

(Barnes 1963: 362)

The lamenting historians represent a respectable group who reflect, no less than Shackle, the importance and the rewards of tackling the difficulties of understanding the individual mind. Although inherently inferential in nature, 'observations' of influence, motivation, intent, and true and false consciousness are noted as obligatory for historians (Fogel 1982: 82). Whether they consider a dualistic understanding of the mind important or not, historians are, however, more likely than economists, as exemplified by Shackle, to relegate to another discipline its explanation. Even Collingwood, perhaps the most outspoken historian in his emphasis on the human mind as the subject of history, designates to psychology the study of some passive and active parts of the individual mind: the 'subject-matter of psychology' is 'the blind forces and activities in us which are part of human life as it consciously experiences itself', sensations, feelings and appetite. 'Their importance to us [historians] consists in the fact that they form the proximate environment in which our reason [the subject of history] lives' (Collingwood: 1946: 231).

Collingwood is among the historians who concerned themselves with the passive/active dual of the individual, and who, in his *The Idea of History* (1946), like Shackle, strongly advocated its importance to his discipline. Collingwood described the dual in terms of 'the inside' and 'the outside' of an event. The processes of history, Collingwood writes, 'are not processes of mere events but processes of actions, which have an inner side, consisting of processes of thought'. The 'inside' of the event is the 'process of thought'; 'the outside' is the event as realized 'in terms of bodies and their movements' (Collingwood 1946: 213). Collingwood describes 'the inside', through examples, as the process of thinking by which a person determines to do something, appraises a situation, and considering the possible ways of dealing with the assessed situation, arranges the ideas. 'Man is regarded as the only subject of historical process, because man is regarded as the only animal that thinks, or thinks enough, and clearly enough, to render his actions the expressions of his thoughts' (Collingwood 1946: 216). The 'thought in the mind of the person by whose agency the event came about . . . is not something other than the event, it is the inside of the event itself' (Collingwood 1946: 214–15).

Interaction between the individual and society[10]

The dual of the interaction between the individual and society is as complex, if not more so, than the dual at work on the individual scale. To best understand it, despite this complexity, it is useful to divide the interaction into two subdivisions: the impact of the group on the behaviour of the individual and the impact of the individual's decisions and actions on the group. Each interaction entails a different type of dynamics. To examine for economics and history the interaction as one of the individual and the group on each other is to try to seize a social dynamic process of continuous change. But what is meant by the interaction of the individual and the group on each other? Is individual involvement important? Do such considerations affect theories in the two disciplines? In addressing such questions, the notions of the 'individual' and 'society' will have a wider reference than is usually given to them in economics and even in some divisions of history.

In discussions of social dynamics the 'individual' refers to the behaviour (the decisions and actions) of either the private person, deciding and acting in personal matters, or the public person, deciding and acting on behalf of other individuals, as does, for instance, the entrepreneur, commander-in-chief, union leader, priest, government official, doctor, bank manager, or representative of any organization. 'Society', on the other hand, is the composite of individuals responsible as a group for constituting, perpetuating and reinforcing the underlying legal, customary and institutionalized forces of the group, including such things as confidence in the society's currency or its political system, the group's ethics of work and play, recognized relations between those of different ages or sexes, and a conscious ethos of the collective. The forces which define and bind a group are social phenomena not attached to nor dependent on any particular individual and yet they would not exist except for individuals deciding and acting individually to support them.

Suppose a process resulting from the continuous interaction between social influences on individuals and the impact of individuals' decisions and actions on the whole of the group. Suppose the components of that interaction to be separately analysed.

The impact of the group on the individual

The group at a given point in time is the context in which individuals are born, raised and educated. Within that group, individuals are assigned or assign themselves different functions determined by complex historical and social developments. Some individuals perform manual jobs, while others function intellectually; some are supervised, while others supervise; some have many responsibilities to the group, while others have none; some have access to a great deal more information than others, and so on. As a consequence, some individuals have power within the group; others are virtually powerless. It is such diversity of roles within the group which inevitably generates a group structure and identifies individuals as having relative positions within the society.

Habits, norms of conduct and principles of the group are inculcated in its members by every means possible. Its institutional and moral values determine their conditions of work and play and their social relations. The group's internal structure and its relationship to other groups give strong indicators to the individual as to what is accepted and required activity and how to go about it. Consciously or unconsciously, individuals are constantly reminded of what to do, what not to do and where they belong. They are part of a whole whose streams of information flow by them daily, and they become, to a certain extent at least, conditioned by those streams. The influences of the group on its individual members are those forces which predate the individual or whose current strength is greater that that of the individual; such forces contribute to the stability and rigidity of the group and its values.

The impact of the individual on the group

Each individual is connected to the group in a specifically individual way. The general state of the group, not to mention of the whole of the human world, is determined by a myriad of physical and non-physical, successive and simultaneous events. Some of these events happen close to the individual's surroundings, others take place out of sight; some attract the individual's attention, others go unnoticed; some are experienced directly, others are presented to the individual via various channels. The enormous stream of events taking place at any one point in time (or over time) can be only partially captured by each individual.[11] Thus the general picture of the world perceived from one individual's standpoint will not be the same as that perceived from another's.

Individuals are, in part, directly involved in the creation of this stream of events. Their participation in the on-going action materializes in their individual acts of producing, reproducing, consuming, convoking, investing, travelling, striking, cheering, and so on. From one perspective, individuals are seen to be simply joining in to become parts of the ordered social process. From another point of view, individuals are often seen to be contributing to the whole in ways different from those accepted and generally followed. Since individuals are well aware that their actions are being played out in the group, they appear, in fact, to be creating new ways of participating in the group's activity either as private persons or as representatives of others.

An individual's reasoning ability and emotional sensitivity develops, forges and nourishes a particular personality. That individuality is reflected through a person's behaviour; reactions which are not necessarily compatible with the behaviour of others nor consistent with theirs over time demonstrate the individuality most strongly. Although, as has been seen, only part of what is in the mind of each individual is externalized in actions, what is externalized is the expression of that individual. To some degree, individuals are the ones deciding where they will live, how they will spend their time, what to buy and sell, when they will act alone and when not, and with whom they might associate themselves.

The impact and the weight of one individual's decisions and actions on the overall situation in a society can vary from negligible to substantial, depending on the nature of the decision and action taken and on the function and social position of the decision maker. In general, individuals compete within the group in order to obtain a greater share of the material 'cake' in absolute terms. On the other hand, they strive to obtain a better relative position in their society. Since to achieve these goals most individuals will use every means at their disposal (from negotiating, risking, gaming and guessing to cheating, jumping the queue or lying), the diversity of individuals shows itself in their limited and differing abilities and manners to compete within their society.

Historically there have always been some individuals who have felt strongly a need to create wealth, acquire power or seek fame. The need is often felt by more than one individual at a time, and thus part of the impact of an individual would be exercised in the personal struggle for that wealth, power or fame.

Access to information, skill and knowledge all are possessed in different degrees by different individuals. In every individual's case no matter how great is the quantity of each, it is never complete nor perfect. Since access to knowledge is limited, as is access to any other resource, individuals try to obtain and make the best use of the most they can. Further, since their own ability to process even the available information is limited, individuals often act in a state of ignorance (i.e., according to prejudice, habits, or by imitation), believing all along, of course, that they are pursuing their best interests. An awareness of the relative positions within society leads individuals to compete all the more now to be in positions of power. It can also fuel the individual's drive to acquire more information and knowledge, all of which can translate into a stronger relative position.

Even if one acknowledges that it is the decisions and actions of individuals in a society that constitute the actual outcome of a society's dynamics, one cannot also help but conclude that the actual overall outcome is never due to one single individual. One individual's conception of the *desired*, *intended* or *best possible* imagined outcome is never what comes to be in the actual overall outcome. That outcome consists of the sum total of all individuals' desires, intentions and dreams which have actually taken form in actions. That outcome cannot be the overall *desired* outcome of single individuals, since among individual members of a society there are always winners and losers, surprises and disappointments which offset at least some of the expectations of individuals. Nor can the actual overall outcome be the overall *intended* outcome of individual planners, because within any society there are always some plans that do not work out.

Miscalculation, misjudgement, mistakes, untoward circumstances, unforeseen factors, incomplete information, bad strategy, inventions – all play their part in muddling each individual's separate aims. The actual outcome can also not be the *best possible* outcome either, simply because (a) there is no single criterion of what is best which is acceptable to everybody, and (b) even if 'best' could be measured in some collectively agreed-upon terms, because of conflicting interests, imperfect information and exclusive power, some essential opportunities to realize that 'best' are always lost in the process of continuous group interaction. In any society there are always some people with unfulfilled desires, unsuccessful achievements, and a perceived need for improvement and change. Yet, despite this inevitability (in fact, partly because of it), individuals insist on acting independently, in the ever-present hope that next time they might be the ones to get, individually, enough of their way to feel successful. It is the persistence of this individual hope which at some level leads to the perhaps small but constant activity of individuals and a consequent effect of some of their actions on the group as a whole.

It has already been noted that 'the social impact on the individual' is the source of a society's stability and rigidity. The reverse, however, can be said of 'the individual's impact on society', for an individual's involvement in the group results from individual decisions and actions, and is thus rather a source of fluctuation and volatility for the whole. While the fact that certain practices of the group are traditional, already in place, and 'tried and true' weights group activity to have a high degree of constancy, the non-deterministic, creative, and independently targeted aspects of the individual's activity push towards fluidity and changes in the whole. In the real world, neither of these kinds of impacts can be neatly separated; available for analysis there are instead only the results of a reciprocal interaction between the two.

The reciprocal impact of the individual and society

Everything an individual does affects others to some degree, just as what others do, individually or as a group, has a reflexive effect on the individual: that is the fourth dual economists and historians face. Analysis of the interrelation is rendered difficult not only because the actions of the two entities, individual and group, are inextricably intertwined, but also because the driving forces behind the reciprocity of effect are of different natures.

The forces involved and the information signals generated in the interactions between 'the impact of society on the individual' and 'the individual's impact on society' are quite different. In the instance of the former, the forces involved are the result of the decisions and actions of individuals; the information signalled is an outcome of individual behaviour (although it is important to remember that only part of the information concerning individual motivation is externalized and therefore observable). In the latter, institutional forces, the result of whatever is the established order, are at work. The information signalled in this case takes the form of existing social consensus, which in turn is interpreted and understood by individuals according to their function and position in the social structure.

While individual members of a group are intelligent and creative to different degrees, they are all alike in that they are all limited in how much they can know and by how much their reasoning process can help them understand and explain to themselves their material and non-material surroundings. All individuals have incomplete knowledge of the world in which they live. This inability to know everything creates an uncertainty in the individual. It is an uncertainty which is due not only to not knowing everything about one's present, tangible surroundings, but as well to not knowing what others have in mind, or what is to come, or how one would cope in a new environment. Such uncertainty causes insecurity, which individuals strive to alleviate by establishing their own guidelines and all-purpose answers.

Recognizing their limitations, human beings believe for the most part that a purely individual response to the uncertainties and insecurities that life in the world poses is not the best response. Individuals turn to pooling their resources into groups, relying on each other to help grasp the overwhelming amount of information that is available, not to mention to help deal with that information which is not dirctly accessible to everyone. Separately, they communicate their ideas and feelings and try to make their perspectives understood to others. At the same time they listen to what others have to say. The reality that in the group it is impossible for everyone to get what he or she wants is considered to be compensated for by the fact that as part of the whole each is more informed and, thereby, more secure.

The security afforded by the group is predominantly a security for the whole. Grouped together, human beings develop sets of norms (habits, rules, laws of conduct, principles), and with these a whole world-view, which protect the group and the attributes of its existence – for example, its institutions, its position *vis-à-vis* other groups. The norms function for the large number as a reassuring expression of what the group is of which they are a part. At the same time these norms give individuals the sense that the group's social behaviour is regulated. For adherence to the group to be beneficial on an individual level, the individual must feel protection not only from the vagaries of the world outside the group, but also from threatening whims of the group itself.

Individuals, however, also cry for group norms which will afford them, as individuals, protection within the group. Active participants in the group, individuals desire the freedom of individual expression to shape the kind of society in which they live, but at the same time they fear the exclusion or suppression which might result from the expression of their novel or peculiar ideas. Social norms can alleviate or remove that fear. The social norms which come to be established for group or individual protection partake, like any other component of society, of a preserving force. They have a pronounced effect on the behaviour of individuals. This does not deny that at the same time individuals, the originators of such norms, continue to have an effect on them as well as on any other aspect of society.

Interactions between individuals and the group or groups of individuals, whether in a situation of a respected hierarchy or one of an ongoing struggle for relative positions, are all part of a societal dynamics which functions according to relations of cause and effect. It is, in fact, these causal relations which constitute the field of social dynamics. The difficulty of analysing the cause-and-effect relationship of individual on society and society on the individual arises initially because, of course, in any society, its many individuals are involved in all kinds of activities, and decisions and actions are continuously succeeding one another. It is just remarkably difficult to sort out who is doing what when. An observer dealing with a stream of events which has taken place will, in the account of it, most preferably not compound the difficulty of capturing all the action by considering as well the psychological dynamics of each individual described above.

Such a preferred oversight in the analysis of societal dynamics is, however, often exercised leading to two notably damaging possibilities. Although individual psychology is not generally observable to individuals other than perhaps to the self-concerned, it may prove not appropriately treated as the unknown preface of a general, simplified model of behaviour. Also the lack of concern about the individuality of the decision-making process can yield the result, now conventional in economics, of treating individuals' behaviour by aggregation. The emphasis in economics on man–nature relations, in which calculations are possible, has been a catalyst to simplifying the complexities of man–man relations. Economists have reduced economically active individuals to the 'homoeconomicus', a representative unit and a quantifiable entity, which permits, for instance, treating man in the context of nature and rendering operational theories about technological change. Generally economists feel comfortable referring to consumers x1, x2 who belong to groups X1 and X2; individuality of consumers or of groups is not considered, let alone the specifics of time and place.

In economics, although the economic activity of human beings is the main subject of study, a quick glimpse at various schools of thought will reveal in fact that human individuality (originating in the feelings, intuition, gut reactions and impulses which are responsible for economic behaviour) has deliberately been suppressed. The role of the individual in societal dynamics has been reduced to an almost mechanical process. Marxian economics is, for example, essentially concerned with group reactions and class struggles and has obliterated altogether the concept of the individual. In order to focus for ideological reasons on a capitalist economy where one class of individuals exploits another, Marxian economics found it necessary not to dwell on the study of the individual; it chose thereby to diminish, by ridicule, the significance of differences that exist between individuals within a single class. At the same time, Marxian economists neglect the dynamics that exists among individuals of a single class, for to address it would distract from the prescribed analysis of capitalism.

With neo-classical economics the individual was reduced to a representative economic agent who acts consistently according to a set of rules of conduct. Neo-classical economists devised these rules, and also the economic models in which they are operational, based on the Benthamite philosophy that individuals themselves know best what they want. According to the idea of a uniform mode by which individuals pursue pleasure, the actions of every individual can be reduced to those of 'one', the micro 'one', and multiplied to represent those of a group, the macro 'one'. The tautological conclusion is that the activity of each individual pursuing pleasure, as well as the harmony of the group of individuals, is preserved; each 'one' is free to do as he or she likes. By extension, the *laissez-faire* economic system is portrayed as that in which the 'one' can best pursue harmony.

In this approach to economics again dynamic interaction has been omitted, if only by default. To question whether the 'best' might mean different things to different individuals (or the impossibility of everyone's having some of a limited number of the same things) would distract from the concept of the constancy of individual harmony. Here, too, the interaction of individuals might raise the issue of conflict of interest, and in this instance ultimately disturb the whole philosophy of attainable harmony.[12] On the other hand, Keynesian economists recognized the importance of individual interaction; yet their highly aggregate models leave little room for any analysis of individual subjects. Aware of the importance of the role of the individual's decisions in economic activity, they have none the less encapsulated that role in general concepts, such as 'animal spirits', 'expectations' and 'uncertainty'. Keynesians also make distinctions in the degree of dynamism of specific economic roles: investors as a collective express themselves in action; consumers as a group are merely affected by such actions. Portraying themselves as providing a middle-of-the-road alternative to centralized economic systems and *laissez-faire* extremes, they propose policies for some state intervention in the economy to resolve social and ethical problems, such as unemployment or disparities between groups. Despite such ideas they, too, are yet to offer an elaborated theory of individual–societal interaction.

The Austrian economic school is perhaps the only one to have considered individuals as active and interacting with each other, and yet it is averse to theory and has offered little economic analysis of social interaction. The Austrian economists share the Benthamite philosophy of the neo-classical school, but are at the same time well aware of the important dynamics that exists among individuals. Believing, however, that no theory would be capable of grasping the complexity of interpersonal dynamics, they assert that those choosing to model such problems are motivated by a particular ethics and would use the results of their model to justify government interference in the economy (such as through taxation, subsidies or social benefit programmes). On the basis of their views they maintain that while the market does not function perfectly market forces alone can guarantee the most efficient use of resources. The market ought to be left alone to provide the best opportunity for each individual.[13]

Also brief mention of another small but growing group is warranted, the institutionalists, an amalgam of economists whose fundamental views are based on holism as opposed to individualism. Their emphasis is on the important role played by institutions (understood in a broad way) as the driving force in the economic and social activity of a nation. They see themselves as 'historians of economic patterns' rather than as analytical theorists of the components of those patterns. They are most concerned with explaining patterns of socio-economic events within an historical context, denying that the patterns adhere to economic laws.[14]

Not only ideological controversies but also differences in methodological approach continue to drive a wedge between economists of various schools. Divisions exist between individualists and holists, formalists and generalists, and theoreticians and pragmatists, realists and anti-realists, etc. The dominant group is the neoclassical economists, who advocate individualism and formal theories. With the participation of more and more well-trained mathematicians and statisticians in economics, some among the neoclassicists are distinguishing themselves as neoclassical mathematical economists, others as neoclassical econometricians, despite their tacit understanding and pacific coexistence within the neoclassical school.[15] The mathematical economists tend to be more axiomatic and deductive, while the econometricians are more empirical and inductive. In general, both groups have little interest in the issues concerning social dynamics raised in social psychology or sociology, and when they do it is superficial. The individual is treated by all neoclassical economists more like an object to fit a function than like an active, reactive subject, and the individual–group dual is not considered.

Due to their different specific interests and the different natures of their studies, economists and historians have treated the notions of the individual and the interaction between individuals differently. Parallels, but also differences, between the two can be observed. Historians are generally much less liable than economists to assume that the outcome of the continuous dynamics between individuals and society can be considered to be either the multiple of one individual's decisions and actions or the simple sum of the activity of all individuals participating in the process. Historians have thus not required a 'homohistoricus' (at least not until the emergence of cliometrics). Most historians still distinguish Alexander the Great from Margaret Thatcher, the Greeks of antiquity from the Indian bands of James Bay. But this observation does not tell the whole story, for in fact not all historians agree about the relative importance of the role of the individual or that of the group in their task of recreating and explaining the events of the past.

The distinction individualism–holism is also found in history. It is evident in the divisions between political and social history. While it is easy to conceive the counterpart of the 'homoeconomicus', a 'homohistoricus', meaning any particular representative composite of the individual as a social unit (for example, peasant, party-member, soldier, scholar), there is, none the less, a sharp contrast in the treatment of individuals between, on the one hand, those who are concerned with scientific history, as especially the cliometricians, and, on other hand, the rest of the profession. Historians do recognize groups – the army, the peasants, the clergy, and the artisans – but at the same time specific individuals – such as Napoleon, Augustus, Thomas Aquinas or Pascal – are also given considerable attention. Interest in the individual as individual, i.e. in the terms of a private life, is none the less usually quite by virtue of the individual's public life, social status and the important role the person played in the social process. While the individuality of the person remains, the recognition of that individuality depends on a concept of some individuals as representative more of the social unit for the time and place.

Economics and history differ in the degree and way they employ generalized constructs. The 'great man/woman' approach, in which a prominent person is seen to be the cause of significant change, has dominated history writing. Especially in this century some historians are crying out for a new, less individual-focused interpretation. In reaction, other historians warn of signs of a menacing, overly enthusiastic embrace of the assumptions and techniques of the generalizing social sciences and their ideal 'homo', but the pendulum of historiographic fashion does not yet seem to have swung very far from its previous focus on 'known' individuals.

Can anything be generalized in the way both economics and history treat the dual of the individual and society? There are indeed some parallels between the two disciplines. Both deal with a large number of individuals and with groups. Both disciplines are forced to impose restrictions – of detail, time, place, etc. – on the extent of the dynamic picture they are discussing and, therefore, inevitably find themselves giving a somewhat simplified picture of individual–group interactions. Unlike psychologists, whose discipline allows the interest to focus on one private individual, historians and economists find themselves discussing the individual as individual for the purpose of presenting the 'public', socially influential person or, perhaps, in history, the 'private life–public life' connections in the activity of one specific individual. Otherwise, scholars in both disciplines treat the individual as part of a group whose members share common characteristics, characteristics which permit general statements to be made about individuals, at the very least at a particular point in time in a particular group. These commonly shared treatments of the individual derive from an aim common to the two disciplines: they are both interested in explaining events and the social processes causing them.

On the normative side, both disciplines need to recognize then that it is both atomic and organic[16] interactions of human beings within a material context which are at work in the dynamics of the real world. Without doubt, it is extremely difficult for the observer to appreciate all the factors involved in these dynamics, especially as the components of a given situation are not only the observables, but also many non-observables, such as disappointed expectations, unrealized plans, unfulfilled desires and changes of mind. The difficulty translates itself for both disciplines into problems of being able to see and understand the world as it is, without oversimplifying and excessively distorting it.

In sum, of course, any abstraction and its ensuing theory about the world will be simply one partial story of the whole real world. Further, general issues similar to economics and history concerning the four duals are sufficiently strong to reveal that, although each discipline's schools offer something different, the present study need not concern itself with the merits or demerits of each school's perspective. None the less, as the goal is to understand the world better, the conditions necessarily a part of each step of the theorizing process ought not be further confined by a researcher's vague view of reality, generalizing or subjecting it to convention from the start. Discussion of the four duals reveals

1 That quite generally the observer/observed connection goes unrecognized;
2 That the interest and mathematical functionality of the man–nature relationship has permitted it to dominate consideration of the man–man relationship as distinct;
3 That the whole concept of the individual has acquired a very special 'zombified/petrified' status in economics; and partly in consequence
4 That the interaction of the individual and society has been greatly diminished in the face of the difficulties of handling this complexity.

A lack of confrontation of these last difficulties spills over to affect yet another complexity, that of change. No matter whether one is looking at economics or at history, no matter whether one looks at the names or at the individuals, the difficulty exists in establishing what role the xs (consumers) and the ys (soldiers), as well as a Caesar, a Henry VIII, or a Henry Ford play or played in change or constancy. Ultimately, individuals must be the subject of investigation in both history and economics, just as it is equally the case that verification is inherently related to hypotheses and propositions about their participating role in societal interaction.

CONSTANCY AND CHANGE

One principal proposition of this book, that economics and history deal both with matter and human affairs, neither of which can be disassociated from the other through time, has just been discussed. It was seen that while the material aspect has to do with existence and adaptation to the world in which individuals live, the human component has much to do with their decisions and behaviour. Complications to an idealized, generalized, conventionalized perception of the real world all ultimately derive from the fact that the resources of any society are limited and unevenly distributed. Thus, the individuals in any society compete among themselves for its resources. It is also true that societies compete among themselves for the same reason and according to the same methods. Both disciplines deal thus with human interactions in which conflicting as well as compromising activity takes place. These interactions, it was observed, reflect both a certain constancy, as the group's rules and traditions bound the behaviour of individuals within certain limits, and a degree of change, as individuals continue to act and react both within and outside those societal bounds. It is this constancy and change which are of supreme interest to economists and historians.

Whether viewed now or in the distant past, society is nothing but a composite of individuals. Day after day a great number of people within that composite repeat individually a variety of fairly limited activities. They work during a period of the 24-hour day. At the end of their work day they have accomplished a kind of work very much like that accomplished the day before. Each one rests, nourishes, expresses and diverts the self from day to day, week to week, month to month and even year to year, in ways that reflect some constancy of likes and dislikes and certain habits, and some degree of acquiescence to a systematic approach to life.

The overall effect of individuals' activities in a group produces the appearance of an orderly system. One can readily observe over a period of time society-wide trends – for example in the consumption of ice cream, the staging and viewing of football games, in voting, travelling, worshipping practices, etc. These social trends are seen to be a part of even longer-term constancies, perceived to be general patterns of the group's behaviour as a whole. Such patterns might be appreciated as superimpositions on the patterns of nature – such as the repeating sequence of Earth's seasons, or life, reproduction and death in plants and animals – such that one might see human activity, too, to be regulated by the natural world. Nevertheless, however constantly or cyclically human beings keep reproducing, sowing and reaping, producing and consuming, motivations for their activities do not follow the laws of the physical world and cannot be explained according to them.

Even though constancy of group behaviour for certain lengths of time is undeniably observable, all the while there underlies it a vital ongoing minute-by-minute dynamics of many different, discrete individuals participating actively. There are an incredible number of ideas, dreams, decisions, plans, expectations and calculations bubbling in the minds of these individuals, which in some societies figure in the millions. Some of that number are realized, some are disappointed, some are modified etc. Individuals' actions, from learning a new language, conceiving new life, moving households, changing the type of work, to trying a new food or other product, effect changes which make the situation at any one moment in time different from that of another moment. The continuing actions and reactions of individuals within the social sphere, with their inconstancy and non-uniformity, can thus induce small changes to the daily routine, but most importantly they can also effect big changes to the structure of their society at large.

Individuals do not, however, even individually, opt only for change. Each person is composed both of originality and vulnerability and harbours both the desire for and yet the fear of change. Desire for change might be the attitude to one's own ideas; fear of change might be one's response to the new ideas of others. Individuals strive for 'better' for themselves (and perhaps the whole of the group) and try to alter the situation to their benefit. That human desire to know more, to find better alternatives, to set challenges, to satisfy curiosity, etc., perceived differently by different individuals, generates actions which induce change. At the same time human beings are afraid of or resist change, for it represents the uncertainty of the new as well as the inherent risk that one might find oneself in a worse position than presently. Resistance to changes envisaged by others is strong, and many individuals will put social brakes in motion to stop them. While the desire for and objection to various changes may come from different people, the two on-going forces 'inducement' and 'resistance' are simultaneously at work in a society and thus make for both actual changes as well as apparent continuity and uniformity.

Reasons for constancy and change can also be seen from a slightly different perspective on the scale of the society as a whole. It can be said that during their lifetime individual members of society focus a great deal of concern on their material welfare and thus on the acquiring of those things (jobs, incomes, food, clothing, housing, etc.) which will provide for what are deemed, biologically or psychologically, necessities. The society, which looks to provide for these human needs, can be quite complex and quite dependent on its individual members, each of whom under a division of labour can carry out specific functions but each of whom is also dependent on others for the satisfying of all his or her needs. Not only is there a great variety in the daily activities of a society, but there are always differences in the activities of any one day: overlapping phases of production, new business starts and bankruptcies, losses as well as gains of jobs, the disappearance of some existing goods or services and the creation of new goods or services. None the less, there is a constancy in the pattern of the society's productive process as well as in its meeting of material needs.

This social activity has constancy in yet another way. It takes time, resources, investment and effort for individuals to get trained, to find employment, to produce, etc., whether as producers, workers, or consumers, and each new arrival tends at any point in time to be part of an endeavour already begun. The fear and anxiety of the consequences of changing direction in mid-course on the part of those already involved in an activity (of losing their properties, their plant, their employment, their sources of subsistence) leads them to stay the course, to compromise among themselves and to extend their fears to those newly arrived. Often it is only the newest members to a group who, not yet valuing what they have to lose over their own ideals, expectations and plans, provoke change within the constancy of their environment.

Social norms are most often the standard against which the desirability or non-desirability of change is measured; in any major change they are threatened. Individuals in a social group have varying degrees of freedom in their behaviour; they are, however, all confined to the bounds for behaviour dictated by the social group. These bounds, while taken for granted by the large number, are in fact created and reinforced by it and thus provide its norms for general behaviour. As individuals exercise their freedom, modification of these norms does occur. Manifestations of individual creativity and desire for change, when they attract a sufficient following, create new norms and modify the old bounds, but this process is very slow, taking place over a long period of time. For this reason, changes in norms, while they definitely are changes, are often difficult to detect in transition and are recognized, if at all, only when they have solidified in a new form. These 'invisible' changes give the impression, however controvertible, of human behaviour as either consistent and uniform or changing 'overnight'.

Changes in the general pattern of activity are due to some degree at least to changes in social norms and are likewise slow. When it comes to the intricacy of such changes through time, the fact that most changes are gradual renders them relatively simple to access. This does not deny that the world of human interaction is extremely complex in its dynamics, but it does perhaps help one to understand how in their empirically based assessment of social dynamics some historians and social scientists, and especially economists, can point to the existence of laws determining them. The overall slow change has proved to make easy the efforts of economists to calculate and extrapolate. It is upon stationary or progressive/regressive regularity that most of the assumptions of economists and historians are based.

Despite the lulling appearance that all changes are slow, some rather dramatic, quick changes, or crises, are known to occur in different parts of society – economical, cultural, political, religious crises, etc. Even in cases of abrupt change in just one aspect of society, most of the other parts of the whole are affected and must change per force. While the whole actually adapts as if there were a continuity between the past and its dramatically altered form in the present, analysts attempt to diagnose the relationship between what came before and after. Are crises natural phenomena, natural recurrences under law, or are they an outcome of the social fabric at a specific time and place? Scholars in both economics and history tackle this question as part of the task they have set for themselves, to narrate and explain not simply the uniformity and non-uniformity of human activity, but also the fundamental causes of changes in that activity. They share the narrative and explanatory part of the historical task. The economist's counterpart to the historian who finds characteristics of continuity in a myriad of 'similar' events, who is preoccupied by the 'natural' course of human events or who detects patterns in the past activity of human beings, has, however, a definite eye on how conclusions based on the past can be carried into the future.

With the help of powerful tools, such as statistics, econometrics and computers, economists are becoming quite good at isolating indicators for forecasting future levels of employment, production, stocks, etc. Yet they have shown themselves incapable of predicting crises. They did not foresee the crisis of 1929 nor what economic changes the end of the Second World War was to bring. They did not foresee the 1971 dollar crisis, the oil crisis, the unexpected and unprecedented rise in the interest rate in 1980–2, nor the stock exchange crash in 1987. Such a string of missed prognoses would lead one to ask if prediction of such events is even possible and how 'laws' function in economics. Is there a difference between forecasting the level of future output and predicting the next major economic disturbance?

Do economists, in fact, even consider themselves to be in the business of predicting major future events? While there should be no wonder that economists are rarely capable of anticipating economic crises, since as a group they are more concerned with seeing general patterns than they are with identifying the causes underlying the 'regularity' of their world, in principle the ranks are divided as to their role. Some economists would maintain that forecasts of levels of production, employment, consumer demands, etc. are merely conditional forecasts. By observing past levels and assessing the state of the present market they maintain, one can quite legitimately assume, that should the course of a thing continue (and given no major disturbance to upset this course, it will), one can fairly easily extrapolate or project into the future. Crises, they assert, are precisely major disturbances which trigger the unexpected, and which are therefore not within the realm of the predictable. They note as well that quite often the factors causing major disturbances are not even economic, and thus, for that reason as well, are outside the economists' field of forecasting.

Other economists simply play down the notion of crisis, arguing that there is a natural course of activities in a market economy. It is because of imperfections in the system, one of these being the societal dynamics discussed earlier, that economic activity periodically heats up or slows down. Such changes take an economy off its natural course only temporarily. These same economists also argue that emphasis should not be put on the temporary anomalies (crises), but on the persisting forces which bring about the natural course. They believe strongly that such a course is inherently stable and that therefore there must be underlying laws which regulate the behaviour of an economy. For them, the task of economists is to establish those laws and to 'predict' the restabilization of the economy due to them.

Still other economists, while they deny the existence of an inherent stability in an economy, claim that there is inherent regularity of fluctuation. Crises are not anomalies at all, but merely the most dramatic points in regular fluctuations. While they insist that it is the business of economists to be concerned with the fluctuations, they assert that the 'crisis points' which should not be of greater concern than any other point in the fluctuation. Their approach is to attempt to explain the fluctuations in terms of patterns, or perhaps even laws. These economists have tacitly accepted the burden of predicting extreme economic activity, if not crises, for as the established patterns of fluctuations repeat themselves, so too ought their extremes.

As a group, economists are clearly most concerned with seeing general patterns. Patterns as such, however, may well be devoid of information about causal connections, and it is no small wonder therefore that economists are rarely capable of anticipating economic crises. As noted above, there are undeniably regularities to be found by economists and even historians, especially in man–nature relations. But what does detection of such regularities mean in economics and history? In material relations there seems to be an identifiable pattern of diminishing marginal productivity as one factor of production increases while other factors remain constant; also, in relations dictated by human behaviour there seems indeed to be a general correlation between the changes in prices in relation to quantities supplied and demanded, or a pattern of diminishing marginal utility as successive quantities of goods are consumed. Indeed, one knows by experience that the satisfaction of consuming any food, even caviar, without cease diminishes as additional quantities are increasingly available. More and more chefs in an non-expandable kitchen will eventually diminish the productivity of a restaurant.

Such regularities appear to be so consistent in their quantitative and qualitative aspects, in fact, that they are spoken of as if they were the result of elements bound together by law – for example, the law of supply and demand. If it is assumed, and it is rather widely, that specific elements in certain material and human situations do remain in a constant relationship, it must follow then that the relationship in question must hold true in the past, present and future. Do events in reality reflect the 'law' of diminishing marginal utility the same way they do the law of gravity? Can, in fact, the 'real' world be known through a constancy of relationships detected by historians and economists? For example, what does it say about the world to have established that from a set of resources, knowledge and technology for any point in time the maximum production (or other maxima) of a country can be calculated? In most situations, even in the Olympics, realization of full potential is rarely, if ever, achieved.

What is to be done with deviations from regularity in the world, with elements which do not adhere fully to law, or with less-than-optimal outcome? Such discrepancies are presently viewed as error phenomena whose margins are treated with some interest in an effort to detect further sub-regularities. But is reality constantly erring, falling short of the mark, in conflict with its own laws? The conventions for dealing with reality seem to depict it thus. One speaks of a macro-structure of the world, i.e., of a sum of the elements that compose a society, and of a micro-structure, i.e., individual elements. Yet with the elements cast from the start as idealized individuals, ('homoeconomicus' or even a 'homohistoricus'), the macro-structure is based on an idealized individual element, and this is reflected in further frictionless generalizations in the form of the ideal firm, the ideal market, the ideal bank, the ideal army or the ideal country.

At all levels of the idealizing convention, complications of the whole and its parts have been left aside. This simplification cannot accurately depict the world, which is disturbingly complex and not at all smooth. In the world in which we live changes are constantly occurring, producing situations in which unemployment, inflation, income disparities, wars, migrations, elections, etc., are generated. To understand such changes in society, the activity of the individualized elements must be examined. Further, at the individual level, the elements must be recognized as distinct, not characterized without diversity as they are for a 'homoeconomicus' or 'homohistoricus'.

Economics has defaulted its interests to the single *one* of man–nature relations and has focused on the establishing of configurations of correlations of economic activity. Explanation of man–nature correlations or, as the endeavour actually ought to be understood, explanation of the causal relationship of aspects of statistical correlation in man–nature relations, is boosted by the adoption of the methods and the perceived 'inherent lawfulness' of physics. To undertake with equal confidence the investigation of man–man interrelations, the discipline of economics is missing an important ingredient: an understanding of human social dynamics, the way human beings interrelate. If the majority of economists is more concerned with seeing general patterns, and thereby reinforcing the idea that the notion of law *is* applicable to economics, it is no wonder, with the fact that the degree of generalities formulatable about human dynamics is far from the sophisticated level they employ in their analysis of man–nature relations, that they avoid that part of economics. The disciplines of social psychology, sociology and history, while potentially to be mined by economics for their configurations correlating aspects of man–man relations, together provide few, if any, laws of human behaviour in groups as a basis for explaining man–man economic activity.

To what degree, however, ought 'lawfulness' and laws instil confidence in an area of study in economics? Is it not possible that no law-abiding causality inherent in nature is pertinent to economics, just as it may well not be to history? If not, can one even hope to make sense of human interrelations in economics, to be able to disentangle the various forces which cause the changes from those which tend to bring about some stability in human affairs, even generally?

To study the dynamics of the interaction of individuals and groups, economists and historians often choose to discern and study general patterns, regularities and repetitive phenomena. In so doing they often dispense with considering details of the causes and effects of the individual elements which create the dynamics itself.[17]

It will be argued in the next chapter that in economics and history important contributions do not rest simply on the results of approximations extrapolated from apparent regularities but on an acquired understanding of how various changes take place in the social fabric through the identification and analysis of the forces which could bring about changes. Unlike in the sciences, where the causal relations in observed changes are often deterministic and thus where laws can be established, in economics and history the chains of causation which bring about changes are far more complicated and irregular. Social causal relations include individuals' decisions and actions and are often not repetitive, at least not in a mechanical manner. To return to the subject of verification, it follows, therefore, that the use of verification A would be extremely difficult, for it would be left to check the already simplified theories against data and causal relations which have meanwhile been subject to new changes.

Chapter 4

Verification reconsidered

RECAPITULATION AND VERIFICATION A

It has been illustrated in Chapter 1, how, in the last 300 years, the disciplines of economics and history have slowly undergone a move towards scientifization. The change can be viewed as an improvement. Suggestions for a new manner of utilizing sources as well as of conceiving and assessing premises and theories are appropriately aimed at diminishing *a priori* biases and value judgements of scholars. However, under the strong influence of neo-positivism as it persists today in economics and history, an increasing and now excessive reliance on facts, meaning data, has led to an awkward method as the ultimate resort for judging whether a theory ought to be accepted or rejected, a rigid conception of verification which in economics and history can only function as a pseudo-verification. It is not a proper empirical verification *per se*.

In Chapter 2 it has been shown how facts, taken for granted as such although their use as data is simply an extension and reflection of the theory's premises, have boosted the confidence of the scholar towards believing that further like data can be used as empirical support and that statistical testing can provide for the verification of theories as neutral and scientific. In fact, independent of their degree of formalization and any statistical 'verification', in economics and history theoretical premises and the variables selected often reflect the scholars' involvement and are made according to value judgements. In a sense, an unfortunate side-effect of scientifization by appeal to Verification A is the belief that economics and history are positive sciences, when in fact most apparently positive statements in economics and history contain normative content. It is not surprising that polarization in different schools of thought persists in both economics and history.

It has also been recognized in Chapter 2 that, for a number of reasons, the most important being the nature of societal interactions involved in phenomena of interest to economics and history, there are tremendous difficulties in conceptualizing such phenomena. Scholars face limitations, such as an incompleteness of information or the complexity of interdependencies to be grasped, at each stage of the theorizing process. Simplifications, complications, as well as some distortions come, therefore, to be introduced. These play their part as the phenomena under study gradually become transformed into an abstract configuration and as ensuing theories about abstract phenomena are perceived through the configuration. To conceive Verification A, therefore, as a test of the theories against the actual phenomena is quite erroneous.

The complexity and importance of societal interaction in events of interest to economics and history has just been described in Chapter 3. In the light of the four duals, it is acknowledged that some arbitrariness in the selection and use of empirical evidence, some normative assertions and value judgements will be found in any study of economics or history. It is further made apparent that the scope of phenomena under study in economics and history cannot simply be reduced to phenomena of nature. Theorizing, by definition an abstraction, when turned then to the workings of the individual alone and in society will, as in all other instances, manifest convenient conceptual shortcuts as well as discrepancies about significant events. Disagreement ultimately about the causes and effects of social phenomena, whether those issues seem to reoccur with regularity or are singular disturbances, cannot be resolved simply by appeal to Verification A to justify one theory or another.

Since Verification A, the direct and once-for-all test of theories about economics and history, is not deemed possible, does that mean that economists and historians should abandon theorizing and verifying? Not at all. Theorizing and verifying procedures in classicism, neo-classicism, Marxism and Keynesianism in economics; and historicism, intellectual history, social history and political history in history have yielded a great deal.

In the present chapter it is going to be argued that a discussion of verification is closely related to one of causality and that much attention has, thus, to be given to the issue of causality in economics or history. Recognition of the particularities of causality in the two disciplines is very significant, especially as a desire for their scientificity increases. In the sciences it is well appreciated that it is only in cases where deterministic causal relations can be established that Verification A can be employed to reasonable effect. Most social forces which are the causes of economic and historical perturbations over time are not deterministic. If a practice of verification is restricted to instances of deterministic causality its application will not only be limited to specific theories, but also its role and contribution will be sorely reduced.

It will be asserted here that in order to have the possibility of applying a verification process one has merely to have posited causal relations. While it is from correlations that theories may begin, they are constructed as theories once causal relations are posited. As such, then, a theory, or 'story' can become subject to verification, or a 'test' of plausibility. In the sciences plausibility of a theory is in large part based on the assertion that 'test will reveal that the posited causal connections constantly hold true because their effects are consistently producable as predicted'. Indeed it is that consistently observed connection of cause and effect which may have permitted the scientific theory to have been established initially.

Like other theoreticians, economists and historians detect and posit specific causal relations. They look to the world of the past for correlations and, further, for evidence of causally connected bits and pieces which they then link together in a theoretical construct. Their exercise of positing causal connections is different from that of many scientists, in that economists and historians cannot turn to repeatability 'on command' to affirm that causality is at work. The causality they posit is the connection which they assert to have been true at a particular place and time. What leads them to be able to assert that it was indeed an effect is in fact no different from what leads anyone to think something happened because of something else – a reasoned guess.

The ability to 'guess reasonably' at the existence of specific causal connections depends for economists and historians on what Veyne calls 'talent'. Common sense, experience and intuition are all components of that talent. Verification, adopted from the sciences, can at best be the checking of the 'reasonableness', or plausibility, of the asserted causal theory. In the verification process, then, further explanation and documentation or a reassessment of the evidence (especially if acquired through analogical or circumstantial reasoning), might be sought. As has been seen earlier, this type of checking is often accompanied by the theoretician's protest, for when the plausibility of an economist's or historian's theory is questioned it is in effect the individual's 'talent' that is opened to scrutiny.

Over the years economists more than historians have been concerned with quantification. In this chapter, drawing heavily on the case of economics, it will be shown that configurations of quantified correlations among specific key variables are observed to occur and often even to reoccur. Nevertheless, it is recognized that it is still is not possible to infer from correlation that causality is at work, as might be done in some sciences. In history it is has been considered difficult traditionally to establish correlations and especially a repeating correlation of variables, not to mention fixed causal connections among the components. What will be said about economics applies thus even more to history.

Economists are actively engaged in continuing the development of very sophisticated abstract models. They do so by correlating a handful of economic variables chosen from a well-established, shared configuration. Each scholar concentrates on a selection of components in the configuration and employs a counterfactual approach using the indispensable clause '*ceteris paribus*': 'What would happen if one variable were to change by so much when everything else remains constant?' By calculation, simulation and estimation, scenarios and alternatives are provided on which explanations and/or predictions are then based. While prediction may and explanation must depend on a (causal) theory, in many cases the absence of a causal explanation goes unnoticed in the jump from correlation to asserted causal relation.

The real challenge for economists, if their purpose is to explain changes in the actual world, lies not only in answering counterfactual questions, but also in explaining how, when and why disturbances in the actual world occur. Moreover, with the help of the correlation of several variables in a configuration, economists could continue from a theoretical conclusion of initial cause and effect to ask whether and how effects become causes of chain reactions and effect other components of the configuration. Which cause/effect/cause might or might not create chain reactions? How do economic disturbances activate, slow, or sustain economic activity at specific levels? There are many questions for economists to answer once they adopt the challenge of explaining.

It is further argued here that it is disturbances which reveal, if not trigger, a specific chain of causal relations. Causal links might differ and be quite specific in time and place within the context of a set of constant correlations among components of a known configuration. Unlike the set of correlated relations which might remain stable, causal changes have a dynamics of their own. In the case of phenomena of economic and historical interest, in which societal interactions are involved, chains of causality affecting variables do not necessarily follow repetitive patterns. The task to understand causality in this context is not an easy one.

EVIDENCE, VERIFICATION B AND THE HISTORICAL CONTEXT

With what kind of evidence do economists and historians deal when they concern themselves with verifying theories? Consider the following general statements:

1 An increase in the temperature of a gas causes its volume to expand.
2 Inflation results from changes in the monetary supply.
3 The European revolutions of the seventeenth and eighteenth centuries were brought about by dissent in the bourgeoisie.

While the third general statement is about past events, the other two examples seem to refer to the past and present. If one were to verify these three statements the procedures would be quite different. A scientist would find no difficulty in setting up an experiment to check the first statement, whereas an economist might find it quite difficult to ask a national finance minister to increase his country's money supply to test whether inflation ensues and further to ask the minister to repeat the experiment to make sure that what first ensued is always the case. It would be even more absurd to contemplate rerunning the seventeenth and the eighteenth centuries with their bourgeoisie, asking for dissent and discovering whether a revolution ensues. Given these differences, how is one then to verify the second and third statements?

For many disciplines, in the light of the nature of phenomena in which societal interaction is involved and the difficulties in conceiving its changes abstractly, verification should now be recast. As the renowned economist Hicks pointed out,

> The facts which we study are not permanent, or repeatable, like the facts of the natural sciences; they change incessantly, and change without repetition.... We are trying to detect general patterns amid the mass of absorbing detail; shapes that repeat among the details that do not repeat.
>
> (Hicks 1976: 218)

And, hence, an extremely flexible method of verification, of intermeshing theoretical conclusions and new evidence, must be adopted as the fifth step of 'scientific' methodology described in Chapter 1. Identified from the start as Verification B, it consists of an interactive process whereby the theoretical conclusion and the selection of empirical evidence, both old and new, undergo change in the light of one another. This process is undertaken in order

1 To find out whether 'new' evidence can help the scholar get a sense of the reliability[1] of the theoretical conclusion;
2 To permit sense to be made of the fact that certain phenomena in the observed world are specified in the theory as regularities and others as irregularities; and
3 To suggest a plausible story encompassing theory and data.

Whatever the initial results of Verification B in the light of these purposes, there would be no grounds to suggest that the conclusion of the theory under discussion is true all the time, everywhere.

Verification B would, in fact, include much reciprocal examination of a given theory (or conclusion) and data chosen, in the case of economics, from the ever-changing stream of indices about persisting or aberrant phenomena, or, in the case of history, from information not previously considered in the light of the conclusion. Ongoing intermeshing of theoretical entities and observational data is called for in order to improve, complete or revise both the theory (its premises, its model, maybe even the way the hypothesis is stated), as well as the empirical data (in their form as evidence or documentation, statistical presentation, etc.). Ongoing discussion may well also reveal that certain conclusions may hold at specific contexts or periods, although not in others. The exercise of verifying the conclusion will very likely extend back to rethinking every component of the theory, from its initial data to the correlations among variables or characteristics to the causal relations among them.

In what sense do statements about correlations among a set of variables or a series of characteristics pertinent to patterns of behaviour or process differ from theories suggesting causal relations?

MULTIPLE AND CHANGING CAUSES, CHANGING DATA AND PERSISTING PHENOMENA

It has already been explained in Chapter 3 how economic, social and political activities are said to be constantly changing. As a result of both man–nature and man–man relations, two opposite forces (individuals' desires, drives and competition, which push for improvement, and their fears and uncertainties, which try to maintain the status quo) are constantly at work. It has been suggested that frictions in societal interactions can result in mild or violent crises from time to time, but that change is determined predominantly by a slow, gradual process. Change is generally perceived as slow and gradual, for most often the individuals in a society as well as the society as a whole are able to respond without undue stress to whatever has altered in the circumstances – for example, social consensus on an issue, or the reallocation or redistribution of wealth, power, or prestige. Simultaneous to slow, gradual change one might also observe, however, swings up and down (without strict similarity of intensity, amplitude or periodicity) in a number of activities, taking the form, for example, of recessions and prosperities, peace and hostilities, the rises and falls of civilizations, political regimes or parties. A perception of swings has led many economists and historians to believe in the existence of patterns which within the ongoing constancy of change exhibit some recurrent deviations.

Economists and historians are concerned with the continuous flow of events in time. In the midst of on-going multitude changes it has become tempting for many economists and some historians to try first to establish constant correlations between characteristics of phenomena of interest which tend to repeat and then to try to identify causal links between those characteristics such that the various changes will be seen to occur according to causality in the correlated fashion. Often in such an approach what is considered to be a causal link between changes or events consists in a loose connection of successive happenings, in which 'cause/because' and 'when' are synonymous. For example, the stock exchange market index fell because the President entered hospital for a check-up; when is causality at work between the two events? Whether theories are

undertaken to explain single events, occurrences which are parts of
cyclic fluctuations or sustained connections, the distinction between
correlation and causality merits closer attention in economics and in
history. One does well to ask first then, what is meant by causality?

A quick glimpse at the literature reveals that causality is a
controversial concept which divides not only philosophers but also
scholars in other disciplines. Recently, statisticians and econometricians have become interested in the notion of causality. The
statistician Holland itemized some of the concerns which arise when
dealing with cause (C) and effect (E) relations:

> One difficulty that arises in talking about causation is the variety
> of questions that are subsumed under the heading. Some authors
> focus on the ultimate meaningfulness of the notion of causation.
> Others are concerned with deducing the causes of a given effect.
> Still others are interested in understanding the details of causal
> mechanisms. The emphasis here will be on *measuring the effects of
> causes* because this seems to be a place where statistics, which is
> concerned with measurement, has contributions to make.
>
> (Holland 1986: 945)

Indeed, of those concerned, philosophers appear to be the ones
most interested in the 'meaningfulness of the notion of causation'
$(C \leftrightarrow E)$; economists and historians are more absorbed in
understanding particular 'causal mechanisms' $(\rightarrow C \rightarrow E \rightarrow C \rightarrow E)$ and
specific cause-and-effect relations. And then there are those who
have an interest in causality in its connection to other issues, as is
reflected in its appearance here. It seems that, in any context, there is
a fundamental difference between the exercise in which, given a
known effect one attempts detective work to find the cause(s) in
order to construct a plausible plot $(C \leftarrow E)$, and the exercise which
consists in triggering a cause and then observing (or measuring) its
effect(s) $(C \rightarrow E)$. An instance of the former procedure would be in a
case where a death has occurred. One is faced with finding out the
cause of the individual's death and who, if anyone, is responsible for
inflicting the cause of death. In the cause-to-effect procedure one
would begin with a specific cause – for example, the tying of a rope
tightly around someone's neck – and then try to find out its effect.
Holland rightly suggests that it is only in the latter direction of
investigation that statistics can make a contribution to the
understanding of causality.

Leaving aside momentarily the philosophers' 'meaningfulness of the notion of causality', difficulties presented by the idea of a direction of investigation alone are already apparent, and one might ask what difference it makes to the idea of cause and effect itself whether the cause is known before the effect or whether the effect is known first and one works backwards to find the cause. It seems, however, that the issue is fundamental to economics and history. If economists and historians are dealing with phenomena where it is established with certainty that the causal relations explaining the phenomena are deterministic – i.e., the relationship between phenomena corresponds to a law or a set of laws, such that A always causes B and is the only cause of B – then the direction of the causal investigation does not matter. If, however, on the other hand, the phenomena under discussion result from non-deterministic causal relations, as is believed to be the case when societal interactions are involved and the difficulty of determining who is doing what first and who is reacting when to what presents itself then the direction of investigation makes a great deal of difference in the inference of what causes what. Econometricians have recently created some confusions with their contributions to the discussion of causality, for neglecting to consider the direction of investigation, their approach has proved, in some cases, to be quite ill-conceived or inappropriate.

Before a lengthier discussion of this issue, however, one might first return to the meaningfulness of causality. Although economists and historians are primarily concerned with the causal connection between specific events (whether an event was indeed caused by a specific something), philosophers are primarily concerned with what is meant by 'cause' or 'effect'. The philosophical complexity of the question becomes rapidly apparent, as should the ramifications of its answer for economics and history.

Causality in philosophy, statistics and econometrics

The concept of causality has been the subject of discussion and controversies in philosophy since at least Aristotle. It is the purpose in this section neither to review the entire debate nor to enter in it, but rather to sketch briefly the issues and how to understand them in the light of economics and history. Philosophers are concerned with the cause-and-effect relation ($C \leftrightarrow E$). The major aspects of the question have long been what constitutes a 'cause' and what an 'effect' and what are the temporal and spatial connections of cause to effect.

Over the centuries the philosophical notion of causality has become increasingly focused on the 'cause' conceived as that which actually brings about or has brought about a change (or effect). This conception of 'cause' represents but one of the four explanatory principles of Aristotelian philosophy, the efficient cause. A teleological notion of causality (found in Aristotle's final cause), a notion of matter dictating effect (present in Aristotle's material cause), or the idea of the formal potential for the end result being part of the explanation for that result (as is the case with Aristotle's formal cause), have lost their part in the mainstream of discussions of philosophical causality. Instead, the concerns of the successors of Mill and Hume have been with analysing the relation of causes, seen to be such by the constancy of the effects they bring about, and effects, seen to be such by being constantly conjoined to their 'cause'.

Causality has been explored both as a metaphysical issue and as an object of empirical investigation. Both ways of conceiving the relationship of cause and effect reveal that there is no experimental way of proving one's conclusions about the notion. This has led some philosophers following in the footsteps of Hume to avoid entirely the concept of 'necessary' connection between cause and effect. According to this view, a discussion of the relation of cause and effect is descriptive. No essential causal relation is implied in statements such as 'All As are followed by Bs' or 'When A happens B happens'. By the same token, however, such statements can claim to capture only a regularity of concurrent or succeeding events and thereby a regularity or even a uniformity of occurrences: they do not explain causation.

It seems that causation enters into a descriptive discussion of the relations of A and B if the conditions of their interrelationship become specified. What constitutes the specification of conditions has been widely debated with the majority of philosophers (represented most notably by Hart, Honoré, Ayer, Collingwood) adopting a formula of 'conditiones sine quibus non' for causal relations to occur. The difficulty is to sort the 'conditiones sine quibus non' from those which are not such necessary conditions. One view posits that 'A is the cause of B' means that given a set of conditions which occured, only conditions A of that set were required for B to be effected. According to this view, the totality of all conditions which are present is the necessary setting in which A can be seen to be the cause of B.

The margin inside which causality can be considered to function is the presence of necessary (those and absolutely those) and sufficient (those within a particular setting) conditions for the effect to be realized. Thus a looser version of the 'necessary' setting for causation would posit A as the conditions within a certain setting which are individually necessary and all jointly' sufficient. Even in the most rigorous understanding of the formula *conditiones sine quibus non*', no logical or empirical necessity was deemed to be essential. None the less, a notion of invariable and 'unconditional' (Mill) conjoining resurfaces in such discussions, as do concepts of laws and law-like statements, and philosophers have turned to speak of physical, nomological or etiological necessity.

Most philosophers assert that any adequate analysis of the causal relation should enable one to distinguish between cause and effects. To maintain this posture, both reciprocal causality, where A is the cause of B, or an arbitrariness of designating A or B cause or effect must be rejected, under the assumption that such relationships obliterate distinctions between a concept of cause and one of effect. While rejecting reciprocity and arbitrariness a philosopher need not, however, obligatorily adopt a conviction that cause always precedes effect. Contemporaneous causality is compatible with the view of a necessary distinction between cause and effect.

It seems that philosophers are divided as to whether by 'causation' one means only deterministic or both deterministic and non-deterministic causal relation.[2] Even though 'causal determinism asserts that *everything* happens according to the causal law' (Bunge 1959: 4), 'a study of causality need not presuppose causal determinism, or even use it as a regulative idea' (Mackie 1980: 231). In the first interpretation a law is implied, whereas in the latter there is not necessarily reference to a law. For the purpose of the present study causality will be understood in the following way.

If a cause or a set of causes can be identified and proved to be always the generator of the same effect a *deterministic causal relation* can be said to exist and one can establish a causal law: 'The same cause always produces the same effect' (Bunge 1959). Take, for example, the popular form of the law of gravity: if one releases an object in mid-air, under the attraction of the earth, always the object will fall towards it. It is advanced here that causal relations need not be deterministic. *Non-deterministic causal relations* are those in which an effect is identified in relation to its non-deterministic cause. While the lack of a deterministic relation does not rule out causation, that causation may have more than one form.[3]

In economic and historical phenomena in which societal interactions are involved, one must begin well before the question of whether the cause and effect are deterministically or non-deterministically linked and reflect on what it means to ask the question 'what causes what?' Unlike the case of a death, where there is a definitiveness about the identity of the 'effect' and the 'cause', in the on-going processes of economic and historical phenomena it is extremely difficult not only to disentangle causes from their effects but also to define what is a cause and what an effect. It is also difficult to pinpoint a change in a phenomenon's role from 'cause effecting another change' to 'effect or result of a previous change'. Clues are to be found only by hair-splitting scrutiny of unveiled details in a stream of related events, specific only as to time and place. What, for example, would be the answer to the question 'which is the cause, which the effect in changes in the relation of wages and prices?' Even though prices adjust much more quickly than wages one might find that in some cases increases in wages cause increases in the cost of production, and that producers in turn increase prices to maintain their profit levels. In other cases, an increase in prices may cause an increase in wages to make up for lost purchasing power.

Can one speak of cyclical causality and, if so, how can what is at one point an effect act as the cause of the type of phenomenon which earlier caused it? How can one type of phenomenon be both cause and effect? Imagine that pressure from a particular group of individuals, workers, succeeds in pushing a different group of individuals, their employers, to make a decision to increase wages. Imagine that this action in turn leads those employers to make another decision, to increase the prices of their product to justify the increase in wage costs. The second decision affects the purchasing power of another group of individuals, buyers, who might be composed of individual workers from other sectors. They might then start pressing their employers for higher wages, and so on. As a matter of fact, from the level of macro-economic analysis not only is there is an ongoing feedback between wages and prices, but also the pressure for changes in both can be contemporaneous. Throughout the economy there are a large number of wages and salaries which are negotiated independently, but in many instances contracts overlap.

Meanwhile, factors external to the relationship of the immediate variables may also play a role in their interrelation.[4] Prices are often changed to accommodate circumstances in the industry or firm other than wages, such as market competition, conditions of sale, etc. There are also many individuals only indirectly involved who create pressures for wage changes. One can imagine, perhaps, a much more general and complicated economic picture in which now governments and politicians, neighbourhood associations, workers' unions, prisoners' groups, investors' firms, financial institutions, school teachers, church parishioners, consumers' associations, etc., is each one aimed at bringing about the best state of affairs for its constituency. The decision to seek an increase in wages might be arrived at in order to effect an increase in one's income, but it might also be a reaction to pressure from others. Thus, in this example a decision to seek a change in wages can be a cause or an effect.

There may be no problem philosophically in allowing that events of type A can at some time later cause events of type B, nor also that events of type B at some time later can cause events of type A. Further, there is no problem in saying that a particular individual event, say a price rise in this market at this time, was brought about by a number of individual, converging causal chains. At different points or on different chains sometimes an A-type event causes a B-type, and sometimes a B-type causes an A-type.[5] In terms of economics and history, however, the abstract positing of the possibility of such kinds of causality does not satisfy the need of each discipline to pinpoint how the As and the Bs, that function potentially in such and such ways, are in fact functioning, or did in fact function. While the problems raised may not be philosophically significant the difficulties they pose to the methodologies of economics and history cannot be ignored. Even within the two disciplines some of their methods (statistics, probability theory, game-theory analysis) are being used already, in principle, to treat these problems; in practice, however, none of these methods can work when the attempt is to do more than trace single cause-and-effect relations in the past. Given the kind of phenomena of interest to economics and history, it is never possible to know who among the involved will make a move and what kind of reaction the move might have on others in the future.

In the realm of social dynamics, the various actions and reactions will produce all kinds of positive as well as negative effects for each individual or group of individuals and for the society as whole. It is the sum of these positive and negative effects which, by cumulation, will activate or slow down the economic activity and social stability of a society or, by cancellation, maintain the same balance of forces. No one cause is always the principal and/or recurrent cause of a particular change. To varying degrees it is the combination of changing causes, due to changing sets of circumstances, which creates the amplification in one direction or the other, and thus feeds the perceived phenomenon of upward–downward swings or temporary equilibrium. In such a cumulative process not all relations are causal relations, not all changes are caused by previous changes and not all, nor perhaps any, changes in one variable will necessarily and systematically lead to changes in another variable or variables.

The instances of cause–effect relations in economics and history are extremely complex. There is no uniformity of cause and much multiplicity of effect. Despite, or perhaps because of, the interwoven as well as correlated causal relationships of economics, econometricians have recently begun to show interest in the notion of causality. They have devised statistical techniques to 'test' for causality. If such tests are conducted simply as an intellectual exercise they are, while being questionable, not dangerous. When, however, such tests are applied to macro-relationships, such as the causal relation between income and money, and are then used to recommend macro-policies which affect real people in an economy, then the meaning and the validity of such a procedure must be called into question.

Both statisticians and econometricians (see Holland, Granger, Swamy) have recently become interested in the concept of causality. It seems that the statisticians are analysing the place of causality in statistics and have generally been more careful than the econometricians in making the distinction between $(C \rightarrow E)$ and $(C \leftarrow E)$. They point out that only certain cases of the former can be dealt with by statistics: 'It is my opinion that an emphasis on the effects of causes rather than on the causes of effects is, in itself, an important consequence of bringing statistical reasoning to bear on the analysis of causation' (Holland 1986: 945). It is interesting to note that Holland refers to cases in economics even though he was not concerned with economics or history in particular.

Many theoretical econometricians are, on the other hand,

interested in causality, with an eye to establishing permanent causal relations (whether these are probabilistic or non-probabilistic does not change the argument) in order to be able to predict.

> If the goal is to select the best decision from a set of economic choices, it is usually not enough to know that economic variables are related. In addition, we must also know the direction of the relation and, in many cases, the magnitudes involved. Toward this end, econometrics, using economic theory, mathematical economics, and statistical inference as analytical foundation stones and economic data as the information base, provides a basis for (1) modifying, refining, or possibly refuting conclusions contained in the body of knowledge known as economic theory, and (2) attaching signs, numbers, and reliability statements to the coefficients of variables in economic relationships so that this information can be used as a basis for decision making and choice.
> (Judge *et al.* 1980: 1)

Zellner seems to represent the extreme position in adopting an unambiguous, operational definition of causation, which he attributes to the philosopher Feigl: 'According to Feigl: "The clarified (purified) concept of causality is defined in terms of predictability according to a law (or more adequately, according to a set of laws)"' (Zellner 1984: 38). Zellner finds it necessary to insist that this definition 'is adequate for work in econometrics and other areas of science, a conclusion considered to be fortunate, given the importance that the present writer attached to the unity of science principle' (Zellner 1984: 70). Granger and Sims represent those who have developed tests for causality and employ a definition of it in terms of variances.[6] While there is no need in the present study to go into the technicalities of statistical and mathematical testing procedures, the posture of confidence on the part of certain econometricians in their concept of causality is noteworthy, particularly perhaps as it is not universally shared.[7] Dissension is not surprising, for, as Simon correctly pointed out three decades ago,

> In careful discussions of scientific methodology, particularly those carried on within a positivist or operationalist framework, it is now customary to avoid any use of the notion of causation and to speak instead of 'functional relations' and 'interdependence' among variables. This avoidance is derived, no doubt, from the role that the concept of causality has played in the history of

philosophy since Aristotle, and particularly from the objectionable ontological and epistemological overtones that have attached themselves to the causal concept over the course of that history.

(Simon [1953] in Lerner 1965: 157)

Theoretical econometricians have not yet managed to deal fruitfully with the concept of causality and in fact it is doubtful whether their mechanical approach will ever be able to do so.

It is worth mentioning, however, that Conway, Swamy, Yanagiga and Muehlen, in their article 'The impossibility of causality testing', expressed many reservations about the handling of causality by econometricians: 'It is now clear that there are profound problems, both theoretical and empirical, with causality tests. This viewpoint is most emphatically stated by statisticians who object to the apparent carelessness with which some economists equate correlation with causality' (1984: 2). It is the economists' obsession with conceiving all economic causal relations in terms of laws which left Conway *et al.* sceptical and wondering whether anything can be said at all about the testing of causality in economics. Their justified scepticism led them to think that 'those economists who see the object of [the] science as finding the *one* true theory of the economy will find their task difficult, if not impossible' (Conway *et al.* 1984: 14).

Causality and social processes

While econometricians have been debating the technicality of causality testing in economics, few economists, with exception of Hicks (1979), Samuelson (1965) Simon (1953) have reflected on causality. Like the econometricians, however, they, too, would do well to be interested if they intend to say anything about the dynamics of the economic environment. Most particularly they, too, need to be clear on the distinction between a chain of correlated variables and causal relations and to recognize that even when a specific chain of correlations among key variables in a repeated process is established, that correlation is still not sufficient to infer causal relations.

Not only can one conceive, but one can also observe a chain of repeated processes with a succession of different on-going events. For example, days are followed by nights, and yet every day contains unique events; society reproduces itself, and yet in every generation every member is unique; factories repeatedly produce their particular product, yet each product to come off the end of the line represents a distinct occurrence; wars succeed peace, where each period has its own specific events. What, then, can be considered 'the same' in the repeated process? It can be noted that there is the repetition of the process as a whole. Furthermore, one can find characteristics of similarity, or patterns, at successive steps in the repeated processes, or a strong similarity of outcome of the processes. For example, cars of the same model are of the same size, power, weight performance, look, etc.; or the same military offensive strategies can be identified as being used in the battlefields of two or more different wars, etc.

There are also similarities to be found in the manner in which things unfold. For example, in the production of cars, various parts are first produced separately, then some of them are painted, then assembled, then added to the car frame, etc. Similarly, to build a house requires starting from foundations, then mounting a frame, then adding walls and a roof. In these specific cases the steps in the process are repetitive, mechanical and subsequent, and no one would assert that one step 'causes' another. The activity of creating, consuming and accumulating wealth consists in large part in the multitude of overlapping, different processes of that sort. One can, however, distinguish between:

1 The repetitive nature of the *way things are done* and unfold in time (the different steps in the process) – for example, the way houses are built,
2 The changing aspects of *the kind of things done* over time – for example, the kind of houses built, and
3 *The outcome at each step or stage* – for example, housing abundance or shortage.

Although one can establish an order in the way successive steps of a repetitive process unfold there need not be a causal relation between them. For an example of 'the way things are done', one could note that a frame is needed for a house before its roof can be installed 'because' the roof needs a support. Having said this, this does not mean that the frame 'causes' the roof. In the case of 'the kinds of things that are done', it might well be possible to say that due to a desire for greater convenience, comfort or space innovative new construction materials and different ways of building houses have come to be found. In fact, architectural design goes though many changes over time, only some of which pay heed to convenience, comfort or increased space. Convenience and comfort may or may not actually cause new materials to be used. There is, however, always a correlation between them. As for 'the outcome', a builder may find it profitable to build houses when there are shortages because the price of houses then is high. It is equally probable that a vision of profits to be made in housing construction might attract more builders into the industry which, in turn, might yield an abundance of houses. One may find correlations between the profit demand and the supply of houses. One might also find causal relations between changes in population, in profits and in the supply of houses.

The three considerations listed are all related to building houses, and yet one can see that each entails a different kind of change over time and that the succession of changes may or may not be causally related. Change in consideration 1 concerns different, necessarily repeated procedures, whose recurrence follows a regular pattern. Change in consideration 2 is sporadic and cumulative, yielding a staircase pattern. Change in consideration 3 represents an alternance between abundances and shortages relative to demand, and its pattern is cyclical. Thus one can see that an analysis of the phenomenon of the housing market over time entails an understanding of three quite different patterns. This is complicated by the fact that the three are superimposed.

Many other chains of correlations can be conceived. In the discipline of economics, for example, it has been established that it takes investment in the form of equipment combined with labour and raw materials to start a production process. The goods and services produced are, in turn, sold for proceeds, which are then used for further investment, for further production – and the sequence continues. To take another example, a chain of correlations might also be established to describe the components of a state: a group of people with a strong social identity in a well-defined territory, out of whom emerges a leader to represent that identity and under whose leadership a social hierarchy and order are established, with an ensuing social and fiscal cost of that hierarchy and order and, in turn, an increased awareness on the part of the group of the definition of its social identity, the leader's role in that new definition, the strength of his hierarchy and order – and that sequence of correlations continues.

Consider the economic example of production in further detail as encapsulated in Figure 1. An economy is made of a social process in

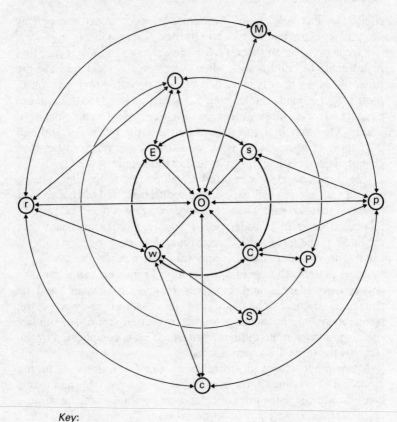

Key:

I = Investment   S = Savings
O = Output   C = Consumption
E = Employment   s = stocks
w = wages   p = prices
r = interest rate   P = Profit
c = cost of production M = Money

Figure 1 Configuration of correlations

which all kinds of produced goods and services are exchanged among
members of that economy. Individuals participate in the economy as
workers, investors and rentiers. Through selling and buying they all

claim a share of the existing or newly produced wealth. Since in a vital economy there is an on-going flow of production and exchange there is, in fact, a repetitive mechanism by which the flow of production and exchange can be described. Economists have discovered and make all kinds of connections between economic variables. For example, it takes investment (I) and factors of production, say labour (E for employment), to produce output (O). There is thus seen to be some correlation between (I&E), (E&O) and (I&O). Investment means physical capital, but it can also mean the finances needed to buy that capital. Thus investment is related to interest rate (r), hence (I&r). Members of the labour force are employed and receive payment for their work (w for wages), thus the correlation (E&w). Together interest and wage payments are considered as the cost of production (c). Here, too, there are correlations between (r&w), (r&c) and (w&c). Also there must be some link between output and cost of production (c&O). Output is sold in the market for a price (p). Some of the revenue becomes the profit of the firm (P), thus (O&P) and (p&P). The level of profit depends on the initial investment (P&I). Individuals consume part of their wages or profit (C); the rest is saved (S). On the one hand, there is a correlation between saving and investment (S&I) and, on the other hand, the level of consumption is related to output, existing stocks (s) and price, hence (C&O), (C&s) and (C&p) and also (O&s) and (s&p). The amount of money (M) available in an economy which permits exchanges is related to output, price level and interest rate, thus (M&O), (M&p) and (M&r). In a functioning economy there are, thus, a variety of direct and indirect correlations – i.e., a dialectical correlation – among all these variables.

It must be said that variables I, O, E, w, r, c, S, C, s, p, P and M are only representative or aggregate variables. At each moment in time (t) there are I_{t1}, I_{t2}, I_{t3} etc.; O_{t1}, O_{t2}, O_{t3}, etc.; E_{t1}, E_{t2}, E_{t3}, etc. That is to say that there are all kinds of investments, labour hirings or firings, or output going on at each moment. This is true over time and also in a cross-sectional analysis at any one point in time. While the actual relationships represented are already very complex one can further complicate the analysis by introducing government, foreign trade and other variables, but this limited pool of variables ought to be sufficient to show how a configuration of some correlations within an economy might take shape.

Such configurations of correlations as the one depicted here are conceived as schematic representations composed of general activities or phenomena which are constant features of the depicted activity and whose relation to one another can be considered constant. While such representations are obviously simplifications they might, none the less, be seen to capture with schematic accuracy the constancy of components of a certain activity in different societies at different times. Even though the dialectical correlation may get more (or even less) complicated, the general configuration remains the same, and it is the general configuration which corresponds to observed components in the actual process. The configuration is independent of time or of a particular setting; the order in which the configured variables precede each other and the way they are related is not specified. Such specification comes about through the conception of a chain of correlations which is, in effect, within the configuration.

Noting the transformation of a configuration into a chain of correlations should begin to illustrate the distinction between correlative and causal connections between variables. Economists have come to establish several different kinds of correlations among the variables of a single, widely accepted configuration of the economy. The most popular approach is that of the advocates of general equilibrium, which conceives the entire configuration as a supply-and-demand setting for goods, services and factors of production, expressed in terms of a set of simultaneous equations. To explain the sophisticated correlations of supply and demand in the macro-configuration, general equilibrium economists have developed theoretical models of the micro-components of the whole.

Many economists, inspired by general equilibrium methodology or by other methods, have also conceived sub-configurations around individual variables, embedded them in turn in sub-chains of correlation and developed sub-theories to explain them. For example, the correlations around I are explained by a specific investment theory, around M by a monetary theory, around c by a cost theory, around C by a consumption theory, and so on. The specifications of the theory are often determined by observing how variables correlate to each other. For example, it is observed that during a certain period a given community consumes 60 per cent of its disposable income. Hence the relationship between consumption (C) and disposable income (Id) is expressed in a simple form as $(C = 0.6 \, Id)$.

Thus economists have developed both very sophisticated macro- and micro-theoretical models of the whole configuration as well as of its parts. They have also perfected the counterfactual approach, which enables them, using the indispensable clause '*ceteris paribus*', to investigate what would happen if a variable changed by so much when everything else remains constant. With calculations, simulations and estimations, all kinds of scenarios and alternatives are provided from which explanations or forecasts are then extrapolated. The importance of all these developments is by no means to be denied. It remains, however, that if the purpose of economics is to establish correlations among variables then its goal is nowhere near as difficult as if it has set as an objective the explanation of changes in the actual world.

A theory that attempts to explain how in the actual world certain disturbances affect certain variables in a configuration is not easy to build. Integral in its difficulty is explaining chain reactions, or how some effects in turn cause reactions by which other components of the configuration are affected. To recognize this fully the distinction between correlation and causation is crucial. As seen above, changes trigger chains of causal effects. Even if changes have their place within a configuration and, despite them, fixed correlations still exist among components of the process, it remains that the causal changes they wreak have a dynamics of their own.[8] Unlike the correlations which remain stable, causal relations, especially when societal interactions in the form of decisions and actions are involved, do not necessarily follow any pattern, let alone one of repetition.

If, in relative terms, a chain of correlations is constant and if no changes in activity occur, including no change in the level of activity in each of the configuration's components, in most instances a harmoniously tranquil world would exist now and and for ever. The work of the economist or of the historian would be trivial and not terribly interesting. In the actual world, however, all kinds of changes are constantly affecting components of the chain and producing pressures which make further changes happen in the level of activity. What influence an economic cause has is somehow dependent on the whole economic and cultural context, which, of course, changes over the epochs and across cultures. For example, in the configuration of the economy, whether the changes take place in labour relations, competition among financial institutions or industries, availability of raw materials, political tensions, attitudes towards consumption, investment and saving, they will effect changes in the level of economic activity of perhaps employment, consumption, savings, investment, and so on. These changes will, in turn, feed into each other to produce patterns of behaviour such as inflation, deflation, expansion, recession, full employment and unemployment. Ensuing up-and-down fluctuation in the various levels of economic activity is often perceived as a persisting phenomenon, a perception which has given rise to theories of economic cycles in which the emphasis is put on the repetitive character of the phenomenon.

It is now easy to make parallels with history. Take the earlier example of the configuration of what constitutes a state. Changes in the attitude of the leader, a desire for expansion, a sense of being threatened, ambition of the military officers, civil disobedience or cultural decadence are all possible causes of the rise and fall of powers. The historian, like the economist, tries to discover the causes of what happened by positing causal relations, but unlike the economist the historian assesses particular instances of states in their historical context and predominantly refrains from inferring that one set of posited causes applies to another, even if its occurrence is perceived in some respects as a recurrence (an economist would not hesitate to make such an inference). The rise and the fall of the Chinese Empire is seen to be different from the rise and fall of Greece and that in turn is different from that of Rome, etc. As another example, similar characteristics might be found in the last three European wars, but it remains that their historic importance is still considered to lie in their particularities as events.

Causality in economics and history

Unlike the philosopher, who is concerned with the meaning of causality or the statistician, who is interested in the measurement of the effect of a cause, economists and historians are primarily in search of clues to detecting causal connections, perhaps even mechanisms which might reveal which events cause other events which in turn cause other events and so on. Certain clues, not to mention mechanisms, would enable economists to explain as well as observe configurations and correlations, and historians to reconstruct a sound plot of what has happened.

To assert, for example, in the configuration of the economic system that interest rates and investment are correlated is not sufficient to imply that there is a causal relation between them – i.e., that a change in the rate of interest will always cause a change in the level of investment or that a change in the level of investment will always lead to a change in the rate of interest. In certain circumstances, change in one variable may cause a change in the other, but in other circumstances one variable may change without the other altering at all. It is also not impossible for each to change without having affected the other at all.

The causal relationships of phenomena of interest to economics and history are not and cannot be permanent, because of the nature of the causes which affect the variables (separately or as they are part of a sub-set) in their configurations. The root cause of most phenomena is human decisions. At each moment, individuals or a group of individuals possess a certain amount of knowledge, on the basis of which they form their judgements. As noted earlier, they act and react in a world of incomplete information and uncertainty as regards the future. Individuals go through changes in their expectations, tastes, fashions and any number of factors which will influence their decisions.

Even in a state or an economy where everything is controlled by a central bureau and in which a higher authority can to a certain degree condition human behaviour to follow strict rules, exogenous changes such as technology, weather, natural disasters, accidents, will randomly affect components of the configuration. Randomness will thus still have to be accounted for. In a decentralized system, where the functioning of the whole depends on the participation of a multitude of decision makers, the input of each is perceived as a signal for change or as news to be assessed by others at that moment and acted upon. Individual reactions can either be negative or positive, which means that an individual confronted with similar situations at two different times might react differently, and that two individuals confronted with the same situation at the same time might have opposite reactions and act consequently. Such differences might be seen by an observer as inconsistencies in human behaviour, while at the same time each reflects a single, rational decision of specific individuals.[9] In a social context, individuals and groups have multi-facet behavioural responses. Governments, corporations, unions, clubs, associations etc., are institutional entities, but they are created by human beings and run by groups of individuals. Culture, education and laws are institutional settings, but they, too, are human-made, protected and perpetuated by individuals. Individuals as persons or members of a group often have different combined social functions. They can be consumers of certain goods and services, producers of other goods and/or services, and members of political parties or clubs, or artistic or sports associations.

Moreover, an individual can be a factory worker and a strong supporter of the factory union, but also an investor who has placed some wage savings in financial stocks and a rentier who, owning a house of which part is rented, fights fiercely the local rent control association. Another individual might be an executive in the coal industry, a member of the local church and sympathetic to the environmental movement, while another is unemployed and a member of a punk group declaiming peace and white supremacy. Any one individual will have more than one goal, while many individuals might share a common objective. Due to the multiple-interest involvement of individuals, conflicting behaviours arise all the time. From their own point of view individuals are seen as acting in their best interests; many recognize that their actions do not necessarily correspond to the interests of the community as a whole, nor even to the majority of its members.

To defend their own interests, individuals form alliances. Some of their bonding together is well intentioned and done for a cause, and some of it is purely strategic or selfish; some of it is vocal, some discrete; some groupings conflict with others, some are complementary. The motivations of individuals' and groups' actions are diverse and have different impacts which shape societal activity as well as the activity's environment. It is the momentum of its activity which makes one group more powerful, more dominant or more influential than another. The membership of various groups changes over time. It is the frictions between groups of various interests and the ongoing shifting in the relative power of their positions, fostered in part by inter-generational participation, which maintains pressure for further changes.

This process is cumulative and its dynamics take place within an organic unity, to use Keynes's terminology of atomic versus organic. Many generations of economists following Marshall have argued that for the purpose of research, one can dissect economic phenomena (whether macro or micro) into sub-phenomena and apply partial analysis by appeal to the *ceteris paribus* clause. Now, if one is concerned with establishing correlations among variables then a statistical, a per force atomic, approach to economics seems almost appropriate. If, however, one is concerned with formulating causal theories it is not at all sure that theories about parts of the dynamic whole, taken individually, can be seen to offer any valuable analysis when they are re-confronted with the actual, complete context. Even if one assumes or believes that it is possible to divide the socio-economic world into parts which can each be tested separately then it is advanced that whatever it means to have verified all the parts separately it does not necessarily mean that the whole is verified.[10] If economists and historians are truly interested in empirical investigation then the organic nature of the world is especially relevant to the phenomena under their study. It is impossible, therefore, for economics and history to emulate the sciences in their verification of components of a theory.

THEORY, MEGA-THEORY, META-THEORY

Part of the impossibility of verifying theories in economics and history lies in the fact that no one theory can indeed do what it sets out to do – i.e., provide the whole causal explanation, even of specified events in time and place. It might be worth pondering if in fact the world is not so complex that human beings can never hope to devise an accurate and complete method for explaining it to themselves. Indeed, everyone recognizes that there are an incredible number of things going on; none the less, most individuals hold at least functional explanations of their surroundings which allow them to cope within the melée. Since research into artificial intelligence is not yet yielding sufficient results, nor is any group of 'superhumans' known to exist to demonstrate the inadequacies of human theorizing methods, human beings, including economists and historians, will continue to assume that they are capable of understanding the world around them. If there are limitations which evoke doubt these may well lie in a misconception of the role of the theories, not solely in the ill-suited process of Verification A.

It is clear now that the distinguishing feature of theories from correlations between variables is that causality is inherent in the former. Of theories, only formal ones are of a deterministic nature; in other words, only the activity they describe adheres absolutely to a law or set of laws. Since probably all economic and historical phenomena are non-deterministic in nature,[11] formal theories can rarely be established in economics and history. Yet many theories about these phenomena are advanced as if conceived around an idea of law.

If laws did govern economic and historical phenomena would there in fact be any need for more than one theory to explain the same phenomena? Economists and historians draw their theoretical conclusions from the circumstances they have chosen to isolate into their theoretical model. In a sense economists are no different from some historians (nor those historians from economists) in asserting a formalistic outcome from their theories. The main condition for such an assertion is, of course, that reality is fully represented by the premises and the information that are fed into the theory. Some historians affirm as a historiographic premise that even if the premises and evidence of their theory represent reality as it was at only one point in time, they can theorize formally about it. They assert that were the totality of the situation (past and present) to reproduce itself the outcome of events would be according to the theory. In that sense, law is seen to bind a particular theory, but one theory no less and no more so than any other, and one is in fact left with the original question as to why there exists more than one theory to explain the same phenomena.

Theories do not have to be, and many simply cannot be, formulated to yield a law. Those theories, however, which are built on the assumption, in use in many economic theories, that a law underlies the phenomena it explains, are, of course, conditional. It is perfectly plausible that the conditions derive from the observation of particular circumstances at a particular time. Therefore, when reconfronted with the same particular situation the theory may well be seen to explain its particular circumstances. In history, it is possible that more than one theory, each having its distinct conditions, may have been derived from the same observations. Different perspectives may lead to different theories, and yet when each is reconfronted with the same historical situation each may well apply.

In economics, theories are generalized to apply to any other instance where similar conditions are met. Several theories whose conditions arose empirically according to a set of circumstances, although different, might be appropriate to that same set of circumstances or others with similar characteristics. The determination of a theory's value depends, therefore, not on whether its 'as if' law holds in *all* circumstances where its conditions (statistical, descriptive, etc.) are present, but on whether it is applicable in *specific* circumstances. It should be possible, in principle, for different theories simultaneously to offer explanations of the same phenomena from different perspectives and for different theories to be applicable simultaneously to different portions of the whole.

The answer to the question 'why are there multiple theories?' has been most frequently based on the assumption that a multitude of theories exists, each intending to explain the same phenomena, simply because the one good one has not yet been distinguished from the bad ones. The assumption carries within it the need for a mechanism to weed out the bad from the good. The impossibility of resorting to Verification A to fill that need has been recognized, for the correspondence between actual events and the theoretical ones, as existing or as having existed, cannot be established by test. The circumstances, a historian would explain, only ever combine in the same way once. No one can reproduce them or replay them; one either accepts the explanation given or sets out to find another.

Economists would agree with historians in saying that indeed there is no repetition of history possible for testing purposes. They would, however, assert that one can find a number of sufficiently similar instances which take place or have taken place at different times and in slightly different circumstances, and one would thus be able to speak of the repetition of an event. The discussion might then turn on what constitutes similarity, an issue which, as was seen above, has concerned philosophers a great deal. Of special concern is, for example, how one could test for similarity. Would such a test not be the same as Verification A?

Does this mean that all theories are good ones, that their individual claims to validity must all be accepted and that no sorting between them need be undertaken? One cannot avoid a sorting effort, if only because the theories themselves claim to be exclusive explanations. Verification A has been used to support such claims to exclusivity, while, as has been seen, it provides to economics and history no way of justifying a theory's exclusivity. Having acknowledged the fact that there is not any possibility of verifying, does this mean that there is no single way of judging a theory's worth? The sciences are beginning to confront the reality of the possibility that there is no one way of knowing that a particular theory is the best or the only correct one.[12] Economists and historians must go one step further and recognize that to speak of one best theory or one correct one which explains everything all the time may not really be appropriate at all. What is at issue is to find the theory that is the most appropriate for that particular situation.

Economists and some historians must thus confront the conundrum of how to proceed to evaluate and apply theories without the handy technique of Verification A and acting upon the assumption that not all theories, and perhaps no one theory, concerning any similar phenomena can lay claim to being generally valid explanations. Verification B, with its emphasis on inclusiveness, would serve as the needed methodological tool. It would render workable the suggestion that many of the theories, both long-standing and new, might be appropriate and helpful to explain specific situations at successive points in time or even those occurring simultaneously.

Economists and historians are, on the whole, grouped in schools of thought which each defend a particular theory (or theories) based on specific premises. In the case of the analysis of the French Revolution a political historian might advance that 'decapitating the monarch and reducing the power of the clergyman instated terror and restricted liberty', while a social historian might assert that 'the destruction of the monarchy and power of the church ended tyranny and restored liberty'. Among the premises of the former might be that ruling elites guarantee harmony in a hierarchical order; in the latter, that social order is guaranteed only when the masses are involved. In economics the same kinds of divisions exist in the case of the explanation of the business cycle.

Mega-theory and meta-theory

The mega-theory and meta-theory provide two different ways out of the sectarian divisions and the insistence on exclusivity that rule presently in the two disciplines. A *mega-theory* is a theory that incorporates other theories under the umbrella of its all-encompassing premises. Over and above each theory that is posited to be the definitive one a mega-theory can provide a set of unifying premises which will render the previous theories special cases of the larger, general theory. It is thus a theory whose all-encompassing premises, applicable in general as well as in specific situations, permit more restrictive theories to be the most appropriate within specific circumstances. Attempts to create general theories have been undertaken in the past, but they most frequently entailed the distorting of the premises of the 'special case theories' in order to bring them under the umbrella of new general premises.[13]

Genuine mega-theories have been attempted in the past, most particularly by historians who were trying to see the similar general characteristics in phenomena which have been dealt with in detail by theories focused on particular instances. Such historians glean from intensive work on the particulars the information they require to formulate their own extensive theories (such as L. Stone in his *The Causes of the English Revolution: 1529–1642*, and Brinton's *The Anatomy of Revolution*) which embrace the detailed work of many other historians on particular issuess without denying the appropriateness of such details in particular case studies. Apparent contradictions are enveloped within the unity of general premises. While the concept of establishing such a generalized notion of historical phenomena will run counter to the historiographic approaches of many historians, there may be, none the less, benefit in the exercise of seeking out common characteristics, if only to recognize the distinctive features of different particular theories and to gain greater appreciation for those features. In the mega-theory the general premises are to be no less dependent on the narrower studies than they are on the wider approach to establish their mega-theoretical appropriateness.

A *meta-theory*, on the other hand, can be conceived less as a method of embracing special case theories as of shunting or concatenating rival theories. It tackles the problem of reconciling theories which attempt to explain a particular phenomenon with not-necessarily compatible premises. The premises in such conflicting or alternative theories cannot be brought under the same umbrella. Thus the challenge is to find the commonality of the theories, either by taking their conflicting premises and detecting their common causes or by acknowledging some commonality about the effect that they are deemed to have produced, but not necessarily by common causes. In the meta-theory one must establish an interrelationship of theories based on the recognition of the situation in question. The meta-theory has to have criteria which would establish a way of recognizing the particularity of the situation in question. It must assess sequential effects and recognize when a new theory would be more appropriate and which new theory is best applied to the situation. The meta-theory would adopt individual mini-theories, some of which may be elements of one or more mega-theories, and assess the situation in which each most strictly claims to apply.

Consider, for example, the case from economics of one theory (Hayek's), whose premises include 'government intervention is harmful', and another theory (Keynes's) which asserts that 'government intervention is useful'. In the one, government policies are seen as causing economic fluctuations; in the other these same policies are seen to help to dampen fluctuations. Obviously these theories have conflicting premises embedded in them which may in some instances be seen to have some empirical grounding. There are indeed times when government intervention in the economy is considered by the majority to have made a situation worse; there are, however, other times when intervention apparently prevented a situation from getting worse. It is, thus, deemed possible that under specific circumstances one or the other theory would be the more appropriate.

The meta-theory is not a super-theory, which strictly speaking, integrates alternative theories. It is instead a theoretical mechanism for determining which theories may be the most effective explanations for each historical circumstance. It is deemed to be a way of using many, in principle conflicting, theories by having one take over where an earlier one ceased to be effective. This is considered to be possible even though some of these theories might be built on conflicting premises and though many might claim to explain exclusively the same or different aspects of the same phenomena.

Explanation and prediction

Theories explain – that is, they give causal explanations for the phenomena they have isolated. Economists have led themselves to think that the causality which permits the explanation of phenomena under immediate observation and theoretical analysis is of such a type that it can also permit the explanation of all other 'like' phenomena of the future. As the discussion of causality has shown, this is a vain hope, for due to the non-deterministic nature of economic phenomena and human behaviour the ability of a theory to explain should in no way indicate its ability to predict. In fact, faith in such a hope has clearly not been fostered by the conviction of economists in the causally deterministic nature of phenomena of interest to them, but rather by the fact that their techniques occasionally yield good forecasts. Indeed, when the balance of forces involved in the dynamics of socio-economic activity remains sustained for a period of time, calculations on the basis of this stasis can produce remarkable results. In fact, theoretical knowledge of the past and present may well permit an analyst to provide a projection of known events into the future. A projection is, however, different from a prediction in that it is conditional; it depends essentially on all the factors which caused the events of the past and present to come to pass to be at work in the same way in the future. If the necessary conditions hold then indeed the future will unfold as projected; the trend will continue forth from the present such that the events tied to it will appear to be predictable. In fact, neither the analyst's data nor a scholar's theory will reveal anything about future causes, nor the extension of past causes into the future.

Analogous to conditional prediction is retrodiction, and for different reasons both economists and historians see value in the exercise. For most economists retrodiction is, technically, as it were, the mirror image of prediction. The past provides a relatively handy stage on which to test the validity of conditional projections in reverse. If a theory's assertions can be revealed to hold true when historical data are examined they ought rightly be presumed, the argument goes, to hold true in the future. The problems presented above concerning the presumed constancy of causal factors apply in economic retrodiction as they do in prediction; however, as the success rate of retrodiction is ostensibly higher (at least of theories that come to light and according to the data carefully selected), the tenuous conditionality of the results is far less apparent.

Historians have also used retrodiction, with some examples of striking insight. The technique entails reversing the chronological approach traditionally assumed for the study of the past.[14] Until the twentieth century, historians had examined the past in the order in which it had unfolded. Retrodiction afforded a way of starting from the present and returning to the past. Once the technique came into use its long-standing, unarticulated, historiographic obstacle was expressed: retrodiction implies the looking backward through eyeglasses (presuppositions, perceptions) conditioned by what has come to pass, by the result of earlier events, etc. The assumption that historians had theretofore been able to do otherwise seemed understood. What was thus seen as an obstacle conscious-imposed, became, in addition, for some historians a different lens through which they could focus their questions.

Problems in retrodicting do exist, however, and they are the same for both the economist and the historian; they are in fact the same ones to present themselves to historians no matter in what chronological way they approach their subject. These problems are no different from those discussed in Chapter 2: particularly, 'blindness' before the presuppositions according to which the events of the past are depicted as having transpired and 'dream-vision' when it comes to seeking evidence, such that it is selected exclusively and specifically to confirm the retrodiction. Were it not for their adoption of quantified economics, historians would not have fallen so far prey to these pitfalls as economists have, for historians actually have far more at stake in being 'right' in their explanations of the past. The past is the only sphere of action that really matters to the historian, while for most economists, as noted, it is merely a testing ground for the future. Econometricians, and cliometricians now as well, see retrodiction, however, as a validation of theories which are uncurtailed by chronology and atemporally applicable whether to particulars of the past, present or future.

While in economics and history retrodiction and projection have their conditions and difficulties, prediction, expecially of behaviour, is even more problematic.

... behaviour has both a purposiveness and a capriciousness that makes predictions infinitely more difficult than for the natural scientist. It is for these reasons that our efforts to predict economic behavior – however accurate in the 'normal' case – suddenly become inaccurate when behavior changes its purpose or displays its caprices. The record of prediction with regard to stock market fluctuations, foreign exchange rates, price levels, or even the growth rate of vast aggregates like GNP, is all evidence of this 'distressing' unreliability of behavioral regularity.

(Heilbroner 1973 in Marr and Raj 1983: 30–1)

If economists can come to understand the reasons for the impossibility of prediction they will no longer judge its merits by its random or apparent successes. Their use of projection might rightfully assume a larger role, as, unlike prediction, it can offer an 'honest' functionality to the pragmatism economists inflict on their study. Ultimately, it might be understood that the role of all theories in non-deterministic studies is not to permit prophecy but to increase understanding.

The recognized impossibility of prediction in economics can

release scholars from the need to tailor their theories to a most restrictive end. Rather than abandoning attempts at grasping the future, however, for these may include functional projection, economists can begin to understand them in the broad context of theoretical explanation. At the same time it would be recognized that the role for Verification A, formerly to affirm prediction, is now virtually nil, and that empirical evidence could expand beyond questionnaire data and statistics. The use of Verification B, never intended to reflect on unconditional situations, and less restrictive forms of behaviour observation will, on the contrary, serve well. Verification B is not a concluding step which yields an end product but one which provides complementing theoretical constructs and empirical information to prolong a theory's potential contribution in advancing knowledge. This is not a plea for anti-empiricism, but for a more rigorous and demanding process whereby theoretical entities can be related to and intermeshed with their empirical counterparts.

INSPIRATION FROM ARISTOTLE

A concept and procedure of verification, or an attempt to confirm or check one's affirmations about the world, derive from Greek philosophical thought. The Greeks had incorporated it into their steps of critical inquiry: Aristotle is the root source *par excellence* of later discussions and modifications of procedure.[15] In fact, however, the ideas on verification which have evolved from those of Aristotle share lamentably little with their source. For Aristotle the goal of the whole theorizing process was the acquisition of greater knowledge. There are two distinct steps to be performed for the process he advocated to be complete:

1 Observing the real world and abstracting from it to obtain a sense of and to make statements about its ontology; and
2 Returning from the ontological theory to its reality.

In the Aristotelian learning process, Step 2 is as essential a part as Step 1; the second step does not stand outside the first to serve to confirm impressions or affirmations. Instead, it is the step which gives ultimate meaning to the first stage of discovery. Only in returning to the non-abstract world again does the information collected and organized in Step 1 become truly understood.[16] The real world is made up of objects and their components, each of which serves two functions, an independent one and an interrelated one. Thus if one observes thing x acting according to both its independent and interrelated functions as x' then what one observes is the structure and make-up (i.e., the form), and perhaps even the matter and activity, of x, which cannot be otherwise for x to act as x'.

Step 1 is the process by which the reality of x leads to an abstraction of x as x'. Step 2 brings one to understand in what way or why x as x' must be the way it is in order to function as x'. For example, one observes a dog to understand what it is to be a dog. One then reasons backwards to the type of functions, independent and interrelated, that the various parts of the dog must perform in order for it to be a dog. The crux of this second procedure is the belief in teleological necessity – that something must be the way it is to perform the function it performs.

Of course, the reality which is recast through the abstraction is the reality of the abstraction, but this reality is the *only* reality if the function of x as x' is well perceived. It is, however, not hard to imagine Aristotle's procedure used in a context in which the teleological element is missing. In that case reality abstracted bears a correlation to the individual abstraction alone and not necessarily to any universal abstraction. The reality recreated from the abstraction would bear a necessary relation to the abstraction, but no necessary relation to the original reality which inspired the abstraction earlier, nor to any other individual's conception of reality. Without the teleological component the role of the second step as part of the learning process becomes less clearly essential.

The transformation of Aristotle's second step into Verification A is not surprising nor ahistorically difficult to trace. When appeal is no longer possible to an agreed-upon end for x as x' universal acceptance of the proposition (supported by theory) that x observed is x' in the abstract can only be obtained if x' can be seen to exist in x by anyone who chooses to see it; in other words, it must be possible, whenever anyone chooses, for one to turn back from someone else's abstract formulation and see the instances for that formulation in the real world. In the absence of a universal teleology, agreement among individuals on the correlation between one person's abstraction and the real world is to be found in only two instances. One is in the case of an abstract formulation which loses its importance as one individual's proposition by becoming the generally agreed-upon state of activity of the real world; this abstract formulation is identified as a law. The other is in the case of a formulation which, while it remains personalized, becomes adopted by a group as the best way at that time to 'see' or think of reality.

In both cases, Verification A, a confrontation of x' with x, is imperative for acceptance. In the first case a claim to universal acceptance of one's formulation is made, for it presents itself as the account of a corner of reality and a corner not bound by any particular instance of its existence. It justifies its demand for acceptance by maintaining that anyone who chooses can indeed make the correlation between the formulation and reality – i.e., re-prove that the formulation does represent reality accurately, that x' represents x accurately. In the second case, Verification A serves the same function – i.e., to command acceptance but with less universal results. Here the formulation, advanced initially by the scholar and subsequently by disciples, is presented as perhaps not the only way to abstract from reality, but as the best way to date. In this case x may be x' or simply conveniently, tentatively considered to be x'.

To survive, a formulation needs to be adopted, and the more widely it is believed to 'represent' reality the better for it. To foster acceptance, an individual's formulation is often proposed with guides for its verification. The purpose of the guides is to persuade others that the formulation advocated is indeed the best. The scholar's hope is that everyone will see, via the recommended means of verifying, the strong correlation between the formulation and reality. Verification A serves the role of, at least, urging agreement with a certain formulation and, at most, commanding it.

Without an overriding teleology a theory has no inherent agreed-upon validity independent of its verified status. A theory's existence seems to depend only on its being adopted (for whatever reasons) by consensus. Aristotle's Step 2 has thus become transformed from an extended part of the learning process into a test of what is being asserted as known. As well as distorting completely the function of Step 2, it has been shown in Chapter 2 that this transformation has also detrimentally altered the procedure of theory building. The processes of abstracting from the world and formulating a theory based on that abstraction have been distorted by the role verification has assumed as Verification A. If ever there was one, this is a case of the tail wagging the dog. It is as if the wagging has ceased to be an extension of the animated dog to become the reason for his having life at all.

What is proposed with Verification B is a return to the intended function of Aristotle's Step 2, now in a non-teleological, intellectual environment. The objective of the theorizing process is to recognize the importance of every stage of the process as well as the difficulties each presents. No stage is to be underestimated nor bypassed to avoid conceptual difficulties. It must be recognized that the scholar is dealing with the dynamics of societal interactions. From it the scholar starts and to it the scholar returns. Despite the acknowledged conceptual constraints, Verification B, undertaken with rigour, will explore the most a theory can provide.

Conclusion

A SEQUEL TO SCIENTIFIZATION

References throughout this volume have been made to economics and history in general. The special focus has, however, been on the groups within these two disciplines which advocate quantitative methods and rely on Verification A to validate or invalidate knowledge. As has been seen, quantitative economists and historians claim scientific status and legitimacy within their disciplines through empirical investigation and mathematical and statistical models.

It has been suggested in this study that to achieve rigour in research and to provide reliable knowledge the use of mathematical or statistical models is not essential to economics and history. While in some specific cases such models can serve as helpful shorthand they are certainly not the prerequisite for a scientific approach. It has also been argued that since the dynamics of economic and historical phenomena are not all deterministic, as are the dynamics of the exact sciences, and not always easily quantifiable, they are not necessarily suited for causal analysis in terms of laws nor for study by quantitative methods. Most importantly, given the difficulty of observing the complex, interdependent social activity which produces economic and historical phenomena and their non-experimental nature, it has been stressed that empirical information is as theory-laden as its counterparts in theoretical constructs, a factor which renders Verification A (perhaps appropriate in the exact sciences) inoperative in economics and history, and empirical investigation deceptive by its circularity.

Even while some economists and most historians are conscious of the complex nature of their problems, the quantitative theorists are ironically myopic to the meaning that empiricism must have acquired in the context of their quantitative practices and in their obsession with empirical validation or invalidation. Cartwright is right in stressing how important it is 'to ensure that claims to scientific knowledge are judged against the phenomena themselves. Questions about nature should be settled by nature – not by faith, nor metaphysics, nor mathematics, and not by convention nor convenience either' (Cartwright 1989: 4). Although metaphysics is virtually unavoidable at the foundations of economics and history (because of the ethical and moral values involved), it none the less remains that Cartwright's idea, so appropriate to quantitative studies in economics and history, has not been applied by analogy. Most quantitative methods, as conceived so far, rely on faith, mathematics and convenience to settle empirical questions about empirical issues. Economic literature, and by extension cliometric study, is full of cases where, for convenience, difficult concepts, such as 'rationality' or 'causality',[1] are twisted to suit the intellectual exercise rather than to deal with the phenomena themselves. Model builders continue to insist on the artificiality of their construct[2] and yet willingly prescribe policies on the basis of those very models. The econometrician's insight is seen to be a matter of faith and luck.[3]

Thus, even though economists and cliometricians may be aware of the complexity of their problems they tend to shortcut the difficulties and do so without realizing the severe annihilating impact this has on the empirical content of their theories. In fact, their avoidance of tackling social issues in the broad context, their introduction of distortions conveniently suited to mechanistic theories, their belief that the quantification of all aspects of social and economic activity is the scientific way to go about understanding it, and their excessive concern with causality as relation by law make their quantitative theories unfruitfully self-contained and the empirical content of them redundant. It seems that such quantitative theorists want to have it two ways. They claim, on the one hand, that the only 'scientific' route to understanding economic problems is via the quantitative method and yet, on the other hand, admit, when pressed, that such quantitative models are merely metaphoric tools which do not deal with the real world. One of the two postures must give way.

What is now the significance of these observations? At no point has the purpose of this volume been to advocate turning the clock back on the theoretical developments in economics and history of the last centuries. The scientifization that has taken place has unquestionably fostered the growth of knowledge in economics and history. Scholars do not want to, nor can they, backtrack. The real issue now is, however, the interpretation of scientifization (rigour, coherence, objectivity) in the disciplines in which it has occurred.

A clearer distinction than ever must be made between situations where, in the search for absolute empirical truth, empirical investigations to verify theoretical assertions are feasible and situations where such conditions do not exist. More than ever it must be recognized what a theory can or cannot achieve in each situation. In instances in which empirical investigations can be undertaken to verify theoretical assertions (often the case in the exact sciences), there can be no question of approximations, averages or guesses. Theoretical conclusions about empirical phenomena must stand unambiguously on their own, detached from the theoretical shelter, as it were. Here the process of verification, Verification A, consists in finding the match (or the lack of a match) between a theoretical conclusion and its empirical counterpart.

In the second set of instances (as in economics, other social sciences and in history) the verification of absolute knowledge is impossible, the field of observation is fuzzy and inherent values are not universal. Economists and historians do well to realize that Samuelson was right when he pointed out that no one theory advanced can capture the absolute, empirical truth:

> With better statistical surveys, I expect economists will learn to predict the volume of next year's investment better. With better study of businessmen's psychology, we might further improve our prediction batting average. But whether we can hope to reduce our imprecision gradually to zero is an issue upon which I confess to some skepticism.
>
> (Samuelson 1965: 125)

It is, however, extremely pertinent that the goal of 'zero' should, none the less, be ever in mind; the issue of realism is of great importance here. Realist aims cannot be taken lightly in economics and history, for especially in the absence of any appeal to empirical verification these studies must be grounded in the conviction, shared among their respective scholars, that their endeavour is to understand the world as it exists beyond and without the particular scholar.

Undeniably, the complexity of economic and historical phenomena poses difficulties, but without a realist posture, theorizing about these phenomena towards a common increase in understanding would be virtually impossible. To this end, scholars in disciplines which offer no possibility of empirical verification must develop, as in fact they have, a *modus operandi*. Their working research framework might well include approximations, simplifications and other devices which permit some grasping or encapsulating of the phenomena of interest and hence some understanding and explanation of them. It would be highly inappropriate, however, to make an exclusive plea for any one methodological approach, individualism or holism, atomism or organicism, especially in the mistaken belief that with any particular method, a one-to-one correspondence between theoretical construct and empirical phenomena could be established. Economists and historians can take advantage of a variety of epistemological approaches, since the realism essential to their disciplines is already at the foundation of all the other approaches. To some degree the epistemological postures of reductionism, instrumentalism, operationalism and rationalism can all be useful in the two disciplines, provided they are not viewed as the keys to legitimacy or as an exclusive claim to scientific knowledge. The interpretations of the conclusions from such approaches can be recognized only as at best approximations or purposeful speculations.

A theory is then a mutable set of ideas which is a recognizable unity continuously subject to change. The degree to which a theory continues to demonstrate stability will determine it as sound or identifiable. The fact that a theory is not subjected to a test, as in Verification A, but is constantly undergoing exposure to new facts and new theoretical ideas means that the judgement of its soundness can lie only in a process such as Verification B. Verification B is, then, a process in which empirical information, while an essential part, becomes a complement to the theoretical counterpart in consolidating knowledge.

When Gay wrote of history as a study 'of continuing inquiry' that 'could never be complete' (1972: vol. 4, 165), he could have been referring to economics also. Hicks most recently frequently led his readers to see the affinity between economics and history. In their respective pursuits for knowledge, and especially in their attempts to verify their ideas, economists and historians would do well to continue to emphasize that affinity.

Notes

PREFACE

1 In many instances the importance in the shift of vocabulary has gone unnoticed, perhaps even wilfully.
2 It should be noted that there are, of course, individual economists who are aware of the difficulties posed by the use of quantitative theory. The discussion is focused on a detected general trend, and not on particular individuals.
3 For such studies, see Caldwell (1982), Blaug (1980), Breisach (1983), Fogel (1983) among others.

1 HISTORY OF THE NOTION OF VERIFICATION

1 As the mathematician E. Bishop pointed out, 'This prejudice that all good work must be technical in the mathematical sense, has made economists, sociologists, etc., feel inferior, as if they should mathematize, very often to the detriment of the real meaning of their work' (in Bruter, 1977). See also Machlup, 1961, 173.
2 Consider, for instance, the definition of 'scientific' history by Fogel:

   1 '"Scientific" historians tend to focus on collectivities of people and recurring events', (1983: 42);
   2 '"Scientific" historians lean strongly toward quantitative evidence' (1983: 45);
   3 'The strategy is to make explicit the implicit empirical assumptions on which many historical arguments rest and then to search for evidence, usually quantitative, capable of confirming or disconfirming the assumptions' (1983: 51);
   4 'The ideological stance of a work, the quality of mind of its author, and stylistic merit, which loom so large in traditional disputes, seldom enter into cliometric [scientific] history, just as they seldom enter into science proper' (1983: 57–8).

3 Conversely, the resort to quantitative method does not mean that one is necessarily scientific.

It seems to me that this failure of the economists to guide policy more successfully is closely connected with their propensity to imitate as closely as possible the procedures of the brilliantly successful physical sciences – an attempt which in our field may lead to outright error. It is an approach which has come to be described as the 'scientific' attitude – an attitude which, as I defined it some thirty years ago, 'is decidedly unscientific in the true sense of the word, since it involves a mechanical and uncritical application of habits of thought to a field different from those in which they have performed'.

(Hayek 1974: 3)

4 For example, the German 'scientific' school (Breisach 1983: 203), the Positivist school, the New Historical School (Breisach 1983: 270).
5 For example, Friedman (1953) or Koopmans (1957).
6 Also the presence of Popper at the London School of Economics and Carnap in Chicago certainly influenced directly at least some economists.
7 The excitement for its potential caused the use of cliometric techniques to spread rapidly. As Fogel noted,

The common characteristic of cliometrics is that they apply the quantitative methods and behavioural models of the social sciences to the study of history. The cliometric approach was first given systematic development in economic history, but like a contagion it rapidly spread to such diverse fields as population and family history, urban history, parliamentary history, electoral history, and ethnic history.

(Fogel 1983: 24)

8 The economist Nagel explained the components of economic theory as follows:

Accordingly, an economic theory . . . is a set of statements, organized in a characteristic way, and designed to serve as partial premises for explaining as well as predicting an indeterminately large (and usually varied) class of economic phenomena. Moreover, most if not all the statements of a theory have the form of generalized conditionals, which place no spatiotemporal restrictions on the class of phenomena that may be explained with their help. . . .

In a given codification of a theory, the statements belonging to it can be divided into three subgroups. The first consists of statements which count as the fundamental ones, and are often called the theory's 'assumptions' (or basic hypotheses); the second subgroup contains the statements that are logically deducible as theorems from statements in the first . . . a third subgroup of statements . . . that indicate among other things such correspondence . . . 'signify either various entities that cannot be specified except by way of some theory which postulates their existence or certain ideal limits of theoretically endless processes'.

(Nagel 1963: 212)

9 See Machlup (1955: 3) for more explanation of theories, hypotheses, assumptions and postulates. For a methodological discussion of model see Sassower (1985: 39–72) and Lyndhurst (1976: 1–43).

10 See Malthus (1827), also Senior (1836: 1–2).

11 Even the historian of the Annales mentalité school, Marc Bloch (in Gay and Wexler 1972: vol. 4, 132), succumbed to comparing history with physics: 'where would physics be today if the physicists had shown no greater daring [than historians reluctant to state hypotheses or construct theories]?'. Occasionally, the analogy of like 'sciences' has been drawn between biology and economics or history; see Marshall (1890: xiii); G. Lefebvre (Gay and Wexler 1972: vol. 4, 164), or most recently between meteorology and economics, Marschak (1950: 2) and Theil (1971: 1)

12 This is certainly the interpretation used in the exact sciences, but also that supported by the quantitative theorists who employ Verification A.

13 For the distinction between theoretical laws and phenomenological laws used in this book, see Cartwright's terminology:

> Phenomenological laws are about things which we can at least in principle observe directly, whereas theoretical laws can be known only by indirect inference. Normally for philosophers 'phenomenological' and 'theoretical' mark the distinction between the observable and the unobservable.
>
> (Cartwright 1983: 1)

But for the physicists, she argues, these 'terms separate laws which are fundamental and explanatory from those that merely describe' (Cartwright 1983: 2).

14 It might be added that psychology and sociology seem, with their concepts of deviancy (and their definitions of 'normal' and 'abnormal') to be attempting to walk the fine line between the two kinds of sciences.

15 While Adam Smith is seen as the father of economics, economics began to exist as a discipline only in the nineteenth century. History, with its writers since time immemorial, received recognition as a university discipline somewhat earlier. Cambridge had established a chair of history by the early seventeenth century; the eighteenth century saw historians teaching in Germany, and France and the New World followed suit shortly thereafter. For further information on the study of history in the economic context, see Kadish (1989).

16 Nor was even the appropriateness of the concern always quite so obvious. The second-century A.D. Roman historian Lucian felt the question of how the historian knows about reality in the first place was not really his concern, as historical rhetor, but belonged to the worries of the philosopher. See Breisach (1983: 72).

17 There were, of course, contemporaneous dissenters of various stripes. Halévy's advocating historical study of 'institutions and sects in which these beliefs, emotions, and opinions take a form suitable for scientific inquiry' was a non-quantitativist's approach to collective analysis (in Gay and Wexler 1972: vol. 4, 189), while Chabod simply rejected seeing at all 'how "the secret of history" could be unlocked by the use of "statistical tables, percentages, medians, graphs and diagrams"' (in Gay and Wexler 1972: vol. 4, 245).

18 Hutchison (1977), Chapter 4, has an interesting discussion about such dissenters from this view.

19 For example, the Austrian economists Hayek and von Mises advocated individualism for economics, while Schmoller and the German Historical School professed holism.

20 Some, of course, rejected both – for example, Chabod, who called the search for laws, 'a vain neopositivistic aberration', while eschewing any philosophy of history, historicist or other (in Gay and Wexler 1972: vol. 4, 246).

21 See, for example, Kehr or the Annales school and its *longue durée*.

22 The whole concept of hypothesis was becoming appreciated. The overtures by economists and historians do not reflect their full control of the method, however, and they were often critically mistaken that their propositions were classic *a priori* axioms. For the same issues in natural philosophical investigation, see Clarke (1989), especially Chapter 5.

23 It is interesting to note that had the Physiocrats chosen concrete examples they would not have been open to such criticism of content or method.

24 One of the *trattatisti*, Atanagi, argued that history's lessons were sufficiently true 'to free human beings from the fear of change' (in Breisach 1983: 189).

25 Just to take the example of von Ranke (1973) is to reveal the extent of the interest by an historian in the 'philosophy' of his task:

History is distinguished from all other sciences in that it is also an art.

History is a science in collecting, finding, penetrating; it is an art because it recreates and portrays that which it has found and recognized. . . . To justify our science against the claims of philosophy, we seek to relate to the sublime. We search for a principle from which history would receive a unique life of its own . . . .

(von Ranke 1973: 33–5)

History elevates, gives significance to, and hallows the phenomenal world, in and by itself, because of what it contains. It devotes its efforts to the concrete, not only to the abstract which might be contained therein. Now that we have vindicated our supreme principle, we have to consider what demands result from it for historical practice. . . .

(von Ranke 1973: 39)

Von Ranke proceeds to list: '1 The first demand is pure love of truth'; '2 . . . a documentary, penetrating, profound study is necessary'; '3 A universal interest'; '4 Penetration of a causal nexus'; '5 Impartiality'; '6 Conception of the totality' (von Ranke 1973: 39–43).

26 'Today, however, no one can adhere to any of these [neo-positivist] philosophical positions to any large extent. Logical positivism, especially, even if one is quite charitable about what counts as a development rather than a change of position, had a rather spectacular crash' (van Fraassen 1980: 2).

27 There are a few exceptions: see, for example, the collection of essays in Caldwell (1984) and McCloskey (1983).

28 This is, by no means, the first such attempt to survey the way historians have grouped themselves since neo-positivism, and a number of authors have done so with an eye to a great many more characteristics than the attitude of historians toward scientifization. Atkinson (1978: 33) for example, provides a very useful grouping of historians 'I have tried to select historians

who are "both" prepared to make general pronouncements about their subject "and" relatively uncorrupted by philosophy', according to four distinctions:

> (a) studying the past entirely in its own terms (Oakeshott, Butterfield) or in present day terms (Croce, Carr, Leff); (b) stressing the individual event (Oakeshott, Butterfield, Elton) or the universal law (Carr, though I suspect more a matter of a precept than practice); (c) narrating (Renier, Gallie) or subsuming under laws (Hempel most conspicuously); (d) explaining in rational terms (Collingwood, Dray) or causally (Hempel, White).'
>
> (Atkinson 1978: 37)

29 I will consider the historical work as what it most manifestly is – that is to say, a verbal structure in the form of a narrative prose discourse that purports to be a model, or icon, of past structures and processes in the interest of 'explaining what they were by representing' them.

> (White 1973: 2)

In a footnote to this sentence White goes on to say that Auerbach (influenced by Hegel) and Gombrich ('within the Neo-Positivist [and anti-Hegelian] tradition') have asked 'what are the "historical" components of "realistic" art? I ask: what are the "artistic" elements of "realistic" historiography?' (White 1973: 3).

30 'The past then becomes neither more nor less mysterious than the moment we are living.... For history is an art, like engraving or photography' (Veyne 1971: 229).

31 See, for example, on the side of theory, Gademacher (1989).

32 In conversation with W. D. Irvine, author of (1989) *The Boulanger Affair Reconsidered*, Oxford: Oxford University Press.

33 The empiricism of Pierre Bayle of the late seventeenth century, for example, considered facts 'not as building stones to be fitted into an edifice of generalizations by the method of induction but, rather, as the truth itself. In history "facts" put next to "facts", not subordinated to each other by induction or deduction, portrayed in their sheer aggregation the human past'. It is Breisach's opinion that while Bayle was not right for his time, 'the disenchantment with overall historical explanation in the twentieth century created a favorable climate for a revival of Bayle's ideas, as in the neopositivist views of history' (Breisach 1983: 192).

34 See their contributions to *History and Theory*, the journal forum for such discussions.

35 The work is part of a series *Studies in Cybernetics*, which includes as well *Creativity as an Exact Science: The Theory of the Solution of Inventive Problems* by G. S. Altshuller (1984).

36 Mill's warnings were among the earliest:

> The only mode of direct verification which remains is to compare those conclusions with the result of an individual experiment or instance. But here the difficulty is equally great, for in order to verify a theory (directly) by an experiment the circumstances of the experiment must be exactly the same with those contemplated in the theory.... Although, however,

direct verification is impossible, there is an indirect verification, which is scarcely of less value, and which is always practicable'

(Mill 1950: 340)

37 '*Submission to data is the golden rule which dominates every scientific discipline*. . . . *This rule is the same* for the science of economics as for the physical sciences.'

38 It is now, for example, becoming routine to refer to Keynes' *General Theory* (1936), the most cited work in economics, as 'badly written' because it is in prose and not in mathematical equations. The many subtle remarks it contains about fundamental difficulties in economic analysis are found to be unintelligible by the new generation of economists because they are not translatable into calculus.

2 THE PRESENT PURPOSE AND ROLE OF VERIFICATION IN ECONOMICS AND IN HISTORY

1 The nature of this connection is far from universally agreed-upon. Giere (1988) devotes Chapter 4 to the issue as it pertains to the sciences. See the end of Chapter 2 here for a brief discussion of realism in economics and history.

2 The philosopher seeks in verification an epistemological method to permit the ascertaining, as unconditionally true, of a theoretical statement, such as 'all swans are white'.

3 Two comments might be made here. First, there is a new experimental economics based on the use of laboratory techniques, see James Allison (1986) C.P. Plott and V.L. Smith (1978) and V. L. Smith (1980). Second, the ready availability of data to all endeavours in the sciences is not meant to be exaggerated here, even for purposes of comparison, as not all aspects of scientific experimentation can be controlled.

4 Recurring periodically, the crises were even seen to form a series (listed by Flamant and Singer-Kérel (1968) as the crises of 1815, 1826, 1836, 1847, 1857, 1866, 1873, 1882, 1890, 1907, 1913, 1920, 1929). The assessed similarity of these crises depends in part on the fact that, although they all originated in different circumstances and in different countries, each quickly spread to the rest of the industrialized countries.

5 As Laidler pointed out, 'An endemic difficulty in testing propositions about economic behaviour is that it is impossible to hold "other things equal" and investigate only one relationship at a time. The world does not provide data in such a convenient form' (Laidler 1977: 120). This is just one aspect of the difficulties encountered in subjecting theories to tests.

6 Unlike most econometricians, Hendry at least recognizes, with Einstein, that '*theory models* are "free creations of the human mind"' and independently, that 'models are inherently simplifications and inevitably false' (Hendry 1985: 30, 31). Like all econometricians, he does, however, assert that some models have a great deal of empirical relevance.

7 . . . the inadequacy of the methodology is precisely this: it is clear (and,

indeed, dogmatic) on the quite indisputable point that evidence must count in deciding substantive questions; but it is silent on the crucial and controversial point of *what* is to count as evidence. Evidence provided by the senses? By history? By introspection? By the central Statistical Office?'
(Coddington in Marr and Rajand Raj 1983: 77)

8 'The search for evidence, to be at all consequential, presupposes that what is to count as evidence is itself problematic. For with any interesting theory it is always possible to find some evidence which supports it and also some which undermines it' (Coddington in Marr and Raj 1983: 83).

9 There is frequently a divorce between those who collect, compile and even test with data, and those who formulate theories about the data.

10 The econometricians Johnstone and Stone described the steps essential to econometrics as the following:

The essential role of econometrics is the estimation and testing of economic models. The first step in the process is the specification of the model in mathematical form, for as we have seen the *a priori* restrictions derived from economic theory are not usually sufficient to yield a precise mathematical form. Next we must assemble appropriate and relevant data from the economy or sector that the model purports to describe. Thirdly we use the data to estimate the parameters of the model and finally we carry out the tests on the estimated model in an attempt to judge whether it constitutes a sufficiently realistic picture of the economy being studied or whether a somewhat different specification has to be estimated. . . .

(in Johnston 1963: 5–6)

And

In studying the real world we isolate systems, and apply two methods of investigation. The first consists of making assumptions which can be combined into theories and given a particular form in terms of a theoretical model. The second consists of observing or measuring the components or features of the system so as to obtain a descriptive account of it and can be given the form of a practical specification.

(Stone 1966: 19)

11 'The historian is necessarily selective. The belief in a hard core of historical facts existing objectively and independently of the historian is a preposterous fallacy . . .' (Carr 1961: 6).

12 Consider Hahn's comments:

. . . as I have noted elsewhere the transformation of observation into expectations requires the agent to hold a theory, or, if you like, requires him to have a model. This model itself will not be independent of the history of observations. Indeed, learning largely consists of updating of models of this kind. Although we have Bayes' theorem, very little is known about such learning in an economic context. There is thus a great temptation to short-circuit the problem, at least in a first approach, and to consider only economic states in which learning has ceased.

(Hahn 1982a: 3)

13 The artist feels free to emphasize (a); the scholar must concentrate on (b).

14 '. . . despite its immersion in values, norms, and advocacy, economics should nonetheless attempt to embrace "scientific" canons of procedure' (Heilbroner in Marr and Raj 1983: 35).

15 Such as ordinary least-square, two-stage least-squares, maximum likelihood, etc.

16 Some early economists, such as Marshall, at least, recognized the limitations in using mathematics:

> I had a growing feeling in the later years of my work at the subject that a good mathematical theorem dealing with economic hypotheses was very unlikely to be good economics: and I went more and more on the rules – 1) Use mathematics as a shorthand language, rather than as an engine of inquiry. 2) Keep to them till you have done. 3) Translate into English. 4) Then illustrate by examples that are important in real life. 5) Burn the mathematics. 6) If you can't succeed in 4, burn 3. This last I did often.
>
> (Marshall in Pigou 1925: 427)

17 For example, a regression of two really completely independent variables whose trend happens to evolve closely will produce statistically a strong correlation, whereas a regression of two truly dependent variables may not statistically be revealed as correlated. On the grounds of statistical tests alone, then, an irrelevant correlation can be established, whereas a relevant one, can be rejected. This situation will probably become more and more acute, for the increasing complexity of theoretical problems renders these errors ever less detectable.

18 The present discussion does not intend to denigrate the role of statisticians nor their work, which certainly renders enormous service in providing data and information and can aid as well in analysis. See also Irvine *et al.* (1979) and Miles (1985) for a discussion on interpretation and use and abuse of data.

19 Hicks reflected well this belief:

> It may well be that for econometric work a theory of Professor Samuelson's type is all we need; it gives a superb model for statistical fitting. But for the understanding of the economic system we need something more, something which does refer back, in the last resort, to the behaviour of people and the motives of their conduct. It may well be that ways will be found by which we can retain these advantages as well as the advantages of a mechanical theory; but I do not think that they have been found just yet.
>
> (Hicks 1939: 337)

20 Even if the unfolding present were considered an accessible source of data, the new data would not be the 'same'.

21 In a general way, the problem of macroeconomics – really, of *all* applied economics – is to go from non-experimental observations on the past behaviour of the economy to inferences about the future economy under alternative assumptions about the way policy is conducted. In terms of models, then, we want a model that fits historical data and that can be

simulated to give reliable estimates of the effects of various policies on future behavior.

(Lucas 1987: 7)

22 At the present stage of development of economics, there is an enormous potential for pseudo-testing, i.e., ostensible testing which is, in reality, wholly inconsequential. For example, it is pointless to attempt to test refined, and well-articulated theories with inaccurate or even ambiguous data. . . . And this is not simply a problem of producing reliable statistics; it is a problem of the clarity of the underlying concepts; of what it is that we are saying in our theoretical discourse.'

(Coddington in Marr and Raj 1983: 80)

23 Many writers have warned of the danger of bias in all kind of records. See, for example,

> Historical and contemporary non-scientific materials contain built-in biases and the researcher generally has no access to the setting in which they were produced; the meanings intended by the producer of a document and the cultural circumstances surrounding its assembly are not always subject to manipulation and control.

(Cicourel 1964: 143)

24 See Mulkay (1980) and Hacking (1983) for a discussion on social pressure and consensus in science.

25 It will be discussed in Chapter 3 whether or not the hope of making such a theory-independent contribution is even a possibility in economics and history and thus whether verification would even play a role in establishing a law as such in those two disciplines.

26 Representatives can be found in each of these two disciplines who undertake to understand the world, either for its own sake or in order to make it a better place to live. One might contrast the theorists engaged in purely theoretical constructs with those scholars who devote themselves, for example, to applied development economics in an effort to help the poorer nations, or to a history of the funding of the education of Black Americans in an effort to plead for an increase in assistance.

27 *Without assumptions about behavior, no conclusions whatsoever can be drawn from any set of social facts.* The problem, then, becomes one of discovering the value-component which is intrinsically part of our behavioral assumptions.

(Heilbroner in Marr and Raj 1983: 31)

28 . . . the economic investigator is in a fundamentally different relationship *vis-à-vis* his subject from that of the natural scientist, so that advocacy or value-laden interpretation becomes an inescapable part of social inquiry – indeed, a desirable part.

(Heilbroner in Marr and Raj 1983: 27–8)

29 Those who do not share this method try to replace the teleological principle with a moral principle. For example, they might assume that everyone agrees that whatever conclusion yields the most individual independence or happiness, or distributes the earth's bounty to all most equally, is the most

desirable. Like teleological Aristotelians, then, they construct their theories based on their principles and expect acceptance of them by those who agree with the principles.

30 Perhaps it is true that it is the kind of theory most readily available for examination and comparison, but certainly not the only kind:

> ... given all the weaknesses of econometric techniques, we should be open-minded enough to accept that truth does not always wear the garb of equations, and is not always born inside a computer. Other ways of testing, such as appeals to qualitative economic history, should not be treated as archaic.
>
> (Mayer in Marr and Raj 1983: 59)

31 It would remain to be seen if such 'home truths' in economics and history would be 'applicable at the micro-level', since as Morrison notes, 'the characterizations of micro-processes rarely enjoy the kind of stability exemplified at the macro-level' (Morrison 1989: 15–16).

3   SOCIETAL DYNAMICS

1 There are other ways of conceiving duals in the social sciences. Some of them seem to cut across the four groups identified here. For example:

> The social scientist is faced with a choice: he may attempt either to understand behavior in the actor's own terms, or to impose his own conceptual framework on it. . . . The implication of this dualism of viewpoint are that there may be concepts which are intelligible to the actor/participant (and which may therefore appear in the reasons he gives for his actions) but which could not be translated without irremediable loss into the language of the observer.
>
> (Coddington in Marr and Raj 1983: 81)

2 Veyne includes sociology (it 'is contemporary history or comparative history without the name' [Veyne 1971: 281]) and ethnology in history: 'Historians, in every period, are free to divide history as they please (into political history, scholarship, biography, ethnology, sociology, natural history), for history has no natural joints' (Veyne 1971: 18), while Elton (1970) sees all history as dependent upon the observation of political events.

3 Historians have been known to be sharply divided on the importance of the individual or the group as the appropriate subject focus of their discipline; see Elton (1967) as opposed to Carr (1961).

4 Should history be predominantly narrative, 'to show the unfolding of the plot' (Veyne 1971: 88) or focused on providing causal explanations?

5 In economics, see the axioms of behaviour as laid down in the work of Arrow and Hahn (1971) or the aspirations of Chandler (1984) for application of the axiomatic method in history.

6 See the school of Austrian economics Hayek (1949), Dolan (1976), Mises (1945) or Collingwood (1946).

7 Although in the section quoted Barnes makes reference to the man–nature relationship as one of man–geography (1963: 353), G. H. Clark (1971), among others, has noted the enthusiasm and reserve of historians *vis-à-vis* other aspects of nature, such as the biological organism and the physical mechanism.

8 In regard to nature, events apparently the most irregular and capricious have been explained, and have been shown to be in accordance with certain fixed and universal laws . . . and if human events were subjected to a similar treatment, we have every right to expect similar results.

(Buckle 1857, 1861: 5)

It will be observed, that the preceding proofs of our actions [e.g., murdering and marrying] being regulated by law, have been derived from statistics; a branch of knowledge which, though still in its infancy, has already thrown more light on the study of human nature than all the sciences put together.

(Buckle 1857, 1861: 24–5)

9 There is a large literature on individualism from different perspectives: Watkins (1968), Hayek (1949), Mises (1945). On human action, see Skinner (1972), Benton in Brown (1984), Trigg (1982), Taylor (1985), Giddens (1974), Davidson (1984). The notion of active and passive adopted here is different from that of political and non-political participation (Etzioni 1968: 4). It is much closer to that of Hollis's 'Plastic Man' and 'Autonomous Man' (Hollis 1977: 5).

10 This has to do, of course, with theories of societies. Here again there is a large literature on different ways of defining the dual: Marx's conflict and power, Durkheim's structure and function, Weber's social action and rational bureaucracy, as decribed by Campbell (1981). The same type of discussion is also found in Bhaskar (1979), especially in Chapter 2.

11 Psychologists have written much about consciousness and attention, for example: 'There really is a fundamental fact of attention. The fact of attention is that consciousness is limited. Attention to one "thing" requires inattention to others' (Boring 1933: 194); 'At a given moment a person can think of so much and no more because he has just so much brain with which to do the thinking . . .' (Boring 1933: 198); and 'It seems possible that we cannot attend to two events happening at one and the same moment, and perceive both of them clearly. Thus it was found that it was impossible to take in two pieces of information presented simultaneously, one visually and the other aurally . . . unless the two events can be combined in some way, one must be overlooked' (Vernon 1966: 38–9).

12 Notably, however, some effort to introduce dynamics into the activity of the 'one' has been attempted by applying recent developments in game theory; see Friedman (1986) and Mirowski (1988).

13 The theories they considered the best were those which advocated unbridled market forces – for example, von Mises (1945) and Hayek (1949).

14 For a discussion of institutionalists' methodology see Blaug (1980) and Mirowski (1988).

15 See Hamouda and Rowley (1988b) for an extended account of the history of recent economic ideas and practices within neoclassical economics.

16 The terms 'atomic' and 'organic' are to be understood in the sense in which
Keynes used them in his *Treatise on Probability*:

> The kind of fundamental assumption about the character of material
> laws, on which scientists appear commonly to act, seems to me to be
> much less simple than the bare principle of uniformity. . . . The system
> of the material universe must consist, if this kind of assumption is
> warranted, of bodies which we may term . . . *legal atoms*, such that each
> of them exercises its own separate, independent, and invariant effect, a
> change of the total state being compounded of a number of separate
> changes each of which is solely due to a separate portion of the
> proceeding state. We do not have an invariant relation between
> particular bodies, but nevertheless each has on the others its own
> separate and invariable effect, which does not change with changing
> circumstances, although, of course, the total effect may be changed to
> almost any extent if all the other accompanying causes are different.
> Each atom can, according to this theory, be treated as a separate cause
> and does not enter into different organic combinations in each of which
> it is regulated by different laws.
>
> Perhaps it has not always been realized that this atomic uniformity is
> in no way implied by the principle of the uniformity of nature. Yet there
> might well be quite different laws for wholes of different degrees of
> complexity, and laws of connection between complexes which could not
> be stated in terms of laws connecting individual parts. In this case natural
> law would be organic and not, as it is generally supposed, atomic. If every
> configuration of the universe were subject to a separate and
> independent law, or if very small differences between bodies – in their
> shape or size, for instance, – led to their obeying quite different laws,
> prediction would be impossible and the inductive method useless. Yet
> nature might still be uniform, causation sovereign, and laws timeless.
>
> (Keynes 1921: 276–7)

17 In doing so they reinforce in a sense the popular dicta, 'history repeats itself'
or 'the economy evolves cyclically'.

4   VERIFICATION RECONSIDERED

1 As is the case with any evidence, as Nagel pointed out: 'the undeniable
difficulties that stand in the way of obtaining reliable knowledge of human
affairs because of the fact that social scientists differ in their value
orientations are practical difficulties' (Nagel 1961: 489).
2 This aspect of causality has been discussed by Habermas, Grunbaum and
Margolis in another light, in the discussion of the invariance of nature and
the invariance of history (see Margolis 1987: 240–8).
3 It is hardly ever maintained that the same effect is always produced by the
same cause. All sorts of things can cause wars, or unemployment, or heart
attacks, or whatever. David Hume is a notable exception, but he wanted to
characterize effects in such detail that they almost became unique. See
Cartwright (1983; 1989) for further discussion of cause–effect relations.

4 Many philosophers extend deterministic causality to include the action of many cooperating factors, which together are jointly sufficient, if not necessary, for the effect. They have pointed out that in normal parlance only a few of the factors, those most salient, are mentioned, and the others are just assumed as 'background conditions'.

5 Personal assurance that these situations are unproblematic to philosophers derives from recent private correspondence with Cartwright (1989 and 1990).

6 It is worth recalling Granger's definitions:

> Definition 1; *Causality* ... We say that Y_t is causing X_t if we are better able to predict X_t using all available information than if the information apart from Y_t had been used.

> Definition 2; *Feedback* ... We say that feedback is occurring, which is denoted $Y_t \leftrightarrow X_t$, i.e., feedback is said to occur when X_t is causing Y_t and also Y_t is causing X_t.

> Definition 3: *Instantaneous Causality*; ... the current value of X_t is better 'predicted' if the present value of Y_t is included in the 'prediction' than if it is not.

> Definition 4: *Causality Lag*; ... Thus knowing the values Y_{t-j}, j=0.1, ..., m−1, will be of no help in improving the prediction of X_t.

> (Granger 1969: 428–9)

The definition of causality above is based entirely on the predictability of some series, say X_t. If some other series Y contains information in past terms that helps in the prediction of X_t, and if this information is contained in no other series used in the predictor, then Y_t is said to cause X_t. The flow of time clearly plays a central role in these definitions (Granger 1969: 430). The interest in econometric causality and testing has led Sims and others to highlight an obvious problem, that the choice of which variables to include in the theoretical model may be the prime determining factor of whether test results are positive or negative and in whether, with the addition of new variables, positive test results turn into negative ones. Thus, the separation of the process of theory positing and theory testing is not so clear. See Cartwright (1989) for a full discussion of this issue from a philosopher's perspective on 'discovery' and 'justification'.

7 This is true, even among those who are advocates, as, for example, Geweke: 'The concept of Wiener–Granger causality has proved useful in econometrics. ... Wiener–Granger causality in not synonymous with any of the definitions of causation in the literature of the philosophy of science and would be a poor substitute for those that appear' (Geweke 1982: 209, 210).

8 Here the 'translation' of Cartwright might prove useful:

> We tend to think that a cause (including necessary background conditions) once it is specified fully enough has a fixed influence (whether it operates deterministically or merely probabilistically). But that is not true in economics and history. The influence of a cause can vary from one period or one situation to another.

> (Private correspondence, Winter 1989)

9 This rational capacity is not to be confused with what economists call economic rationality.

10 The atomic hypothesis which has worked so splendidly in physics breaks down in psychics. We are faced at every turn with the problems of organic unity, of discreteness, of discontinuity – the whole is not equal to the sum of the parts, comparisons of quantity fail us, small changes produce large effects, the assumptions of a uniform and homogeneous continuum are not satisfied. Thus the results of Mathematical Psychics turn out to be derivative, not fundamental, indexes, not measurements, first approximations at the best; and fallible indexes, dubious approximations at that, with much doubt added as to what, if anything, they are indexes or approximations of.

(Keynes 1933: 262)

11 A possible example of a deterministic theory would be one dictated by Gaussen's Law of Diminishing Marginal Utility for it seems to hold that the consumption of any good without cease will increasingly diminish the satisfaction of it.

12 'Science exploits a plurality of evaluative criteria . . .' (Morrison 1989: 20).

13 Economics provides numerous examples: Keynes (1936) claimed that his theory was general because it dealt with the situation of unemployment as well as full employment. Malinvaud (1978) developed a theory that he claimed included Keynes's as well as the classical theory as special cases. Hicks (1939) also claimed that there exist four theories of interest rates: the classical, Wicksell's, Keynes's and his own. His was to be considered general, for it included the other three as special cases. Hahn (1982b) claimed that the general equilibrium theory is a general theory by demonstrating that the Ricardian theory as developed by Sraffa is a special case of it.

14 Bloch was one of the first historians to exploit such a reverse approach.

15 The primary textual sources for his ideas have been the *Posterior Analytics* and the *Prior Analytics*.

16 During Step 2 the assumptions of Step 1 will indeed be affirmed or rejected but, according to Aristotle, this is a by-product of the process not its aim.

CONCLUSION

1 Some scholars are aware of the distortions in the adoption of such terms for mathematical convenience. See, for example, Hahn and Hollis: 'Economics probably made a mistake when it adopted the nomenclature of "rational" when all it meant is correct calculations and an orderly personality' (Hahn and Hollis 1979: 12), and Judge *et al.*:

Given the nonexperimental nature of most economic data it is difficult and often impossible to determine cause and effect relationships from the available data. Therefore, economic theory usually has to provide a model that *postulates the direction of causality*. Since many controversial economic theories exist, it would be preferable to examine such models including the causal directions with statistical tools. Therefore, a concept of 'causality' has been developed that can be tested with statistical tools.

Since *this concept is not based on an acceptable definition of cause and effect* in a strict philosophical sense, 'causality' is, strictly speaking, not the appropriate word in this context. *Nonetheless, we will follow the tradition* of the recent literature on the subject *and use the term here.*

(Judge *et al.*, 1985: 667; emphasis added)

2 Witness the audacious statement by Lucas:

One of the functions of theoretical economics is to provide fully articulated, artificial economic systems that can serve as laboratories in which policies that would be prohibitively expensive to experiment with in actual economies can be tested out at much lower cost. To serve this function well, it is essential that the artificial 'model' economy be distinguished as sharply as possible in discussion from actual economies. Insofar as there is confusion between statements of opinion as to the way we believe actual economies would react to particular policies and statements of verifiable fact as to how the model will react, the theory is not being effectively used to help us to see which opinions about the behavior of actual economies are accurate and which are not. This is the sense in which insistence on the 'realism' of an economic model subverts its potential usefulness in thinking about reality. Any model that is well enough articulated to give clear answers to the question we put to it will necessarily be artificial, abstract, patently 'unreal'.

(Lucas 1981: 271)

3 Whether facetious or not, there is some truth about the sad fate of econometrics, reflected in the advice of a leading econometrician: Over a period of about 20 years of analysing empirical phenomena, I have noted down four *golden prescriptions* for those who seek to study data:

I. **THINK BRILLIANTLY.** This helps greatly, especially if you can think of the right answer at the start of a study! Then econometrics is only needed to confirm your brilliance, calibrate the model, and demonstrate that it indeed passes all the tests.

II. **BE INFINITELY CREATIVE.** Be assured that this is an almost perfect substitute for brilliant thinking, enabling one to invent truly excellent models en route and so achieve essentially the same end state.

Failing on that score as well, recourse must be had to the third golden prescription:

III. **BE OUTSTANDINGLY LUCKY.** If one is neither a genius nor a great inventor, this is an essential aid to discovering lasting explanations – by chance or serendipity, despite not knowing them at the outset nor thinking of them in a flash of creative inspiration. Although not every investigator will receive his or her fair share, this seems to be the most practical of my prescriptions.

What advice remains for those not blessed by any of I-III? Then might I suggest:

IV. **STICK TO BEING A THEORIST.**

(Hendry 1985: 29–30)

Bibliography

Achinstien, P. (1963) 'Theoretical terms and partial interpretation', *British Journal for the Philosophy of Science* 14: 89–105.

Adams, H. (1963) *History of the United States During the Administrations of Jefferson and Madison*, abridged edn, 2 vols in 1, Englewood Cliffs, N.J.: Prentice-Hall Inc.

Alexander, P. (1958) 'Theory-construction and theory-testing', *British Journal for the Philosophy of Science* 9: 29–38.

—— (1963) *Sensationalism and Scientific Explanation*, London: Routledge & Kegan Paul.

Allais, M. (1989) 'La science économique d'aujourd'hui et les déséquilibres globaux', paper given at International Conference on Global Disequilibrium, McGill Economics Centre, Montreal, May.

Allison, J. (1986) 'Economic interpretation of animal experiments', in A.J. MacFadyen and H.W. MacFadyen (eds) *Economic Psychology*, Amsterdam: North Holland.

Altshuller, G.S. (1984) *Creativity as an Exact Science: The Theory of the Solution of Inventive Problems*, trans. A. Williams, New York: Gordon and Breach Science Publishers.

Anderson, J. (1962) *Studies in Empirical Philosophy*, Sydney, Australia: Angus & Robertson.

Anderson, P.W., Arrow, K.J. and Pines, D. (1987) *The Economy as an Evolving Complex System*, vol. 5, Redwood City, Cal.: Addison-Wesley Publishing Company, Inc.

Aquinas, St. Thomas (1964–76) *Summa Theologiae*, 3 vols, trans. the Blackfriars, London and New York: McGraw Hill; London: Eyre and Spottiswoode.

Aristotle (1981a) *Posterior Analytics*, trans. H.G. Apostle, Grinnell, Iowa: Peripatetic Press.

—— (1981b) *The Complete Works of Aristotle: The Revised Oxford Translation*, J. Barnes (ed.), Princeton, N.J.: Princeton University Press.

Arrow, K.J. and Hahn, F.H. (1971) *General Competitive Analysis*, Amsterdam: North Holland Publishing Company.

Atanagi, D. (1559) *Ragionamento della Historia*, Venice: D. and C. de' Nicoli.

Atkinson, R.F. (1978) *Knowledge and Explanation in History*, London: The Macmillan Press Ltd.

Augustine (1954) *Opera*, Corpus Christianorum Series Latina (27–59), Turnholti: Brepols Editores Pontificii.

Aydelotte, W.O., Boyne, A.G. and Fogel, R.W. (eds) (1972) *The Dimensions of Quantitative Research in History*, Princeton: Princeton University Press.

Ayer, A.J. (1936) *Language, Truth and Logic*, 2nd edn 1946, New York: Dover Publications.

—— (1940) *Foundations of Empirical Knowledge*, London: The Macmillan Press Ltd.

—— (1954) *Philosophical Essays*, London: The Macmillan Press Ltd.

—— (1956) *Problem of Knowledge*, London: Penguin Books.

—— (ed.) (1959) *Logical Positivism*, Glencoe, Ill.: Free Press.

Ayer, A.J. and Winch, R. (eds) (1952) *British Empirical Philosophers*, London: Routledge & Kegan Paul.

Bacon, F. (1972) *The History of the Reign of King Henry VII*, F.J. Levy (ed.), New York: Bobbs-Merrill Company.

Bailey, C. (1926) *Epicurus, the Extant Remains*, Oxford: Clarendon Press.

—— (1928) *The Greek Atomists and Epicurus*, 1964 reprint, New York: Russell & Russell.

Barker, S.F. (1957) *Induction and Hypothesis*, Ithaca, New York: Cornell University Press.

Barnes, H.E. (1963) *A History of Historical Writing*, New York: Dover Publications, Inc.

Barraclough, G. (1978) *Main Trends in History*, New York: Holmes & Meier Publishers, Inc.

Baumrin, B. (ed.) (1963) *Philosophy of Science: The Delaware Seminar*, vol. 1, New York: Interscience Publishers.

Bayle, P. (1965) *Historical and Critical Dictionary: Selections*, trans. R.H. Popkin, Indianapolis: Bobbs-Merrill Company.

Becker, C. (1955) 'What are historical facts?', *Western Political Quarterly*, 8: 327–40.

Beckner, M. (1959) *The Biological Way of Thought*, New York: Columbia University Press.

Berlin, I. (1961) 'The concept of scientific history', *History and Theory* 1, 1: 1–31.

Bhaskar, R. (1979) *The Possibility of Naturalism*, Brighton: The Harvester Press.

Birke, L. and Silvertown, J. (eds) (1984) *Beyond Reduction: The Politics of Biology*, London: Pluto Press.

Blaug, M. (1980) *The Methodology of Economics: Or How Economists Explain*, Cambridge: Cambridge University Press.

Bodin, J. (1945) *Method for the Easy Comprehension of History*, trans. B. Reynolds, 1966 edn, New York: Octagon Books.

Boring, E. (1933) *The Physical Dimensions of Consciousness*, New York: Century.

Braithwaite, R.B. (1953) *Scientific Explanation*, Cambridge: Cambridge University Press.

—— (1959) 'Axiomatizing a scientific system by axioms in the form of identifications', in L. Henkin, P. Suppes and A. Tarski (eds) *The Axiomatic Method*, Amsterdam: North Holland Publishing Company.

Breisach, E. (1983) *Historiography: Ancient, Medieval and Modern*, Chicago: University of Chicago Press.

Bridgman, P.W. (1927) *The Logic of Modern Physics*, New York: The Macmillan Press Ltd.

Brinton, C. (1957) *The Anatomy of Revolution*, rev. edn, New York: Vintage Books.

Brown, S.C. (ed.) (1984) *Objectivity and Cultural Divergence*, Cambridge: Cambridge University Press.

Bruter, C.P. (1977) 'La formule et le fait', *Economies et sociétés* 11, 3: 532–51.

Buckle, H.T. (1857, 1861) *History of Civilization in England*, London: J.W. Parker & Son.

—— (1904) *Introduction to the History of Civilization in England*, J.M. Robertson (ed.), rev. edn, London: G. Routledge & Sons.

Bunge, M. (1959) *Causality: The Place of the Causal Principle in Modern Science*, Cambridge, Mass.: Harvard University Press.

—— (1962) *Causality and Modern Science*, 3rd edn 1979, New York: Dover Publications, Inc.

—— (ed.) (1967a) *Scientific Research I: The Search for System*, New York: Springer-Verlag Inc.

—— (ed.) (1967b) *Scientific Research II: The Search for Truth*, New York: Springer-Verlag Inc.

Burns, A.F. (1952) 'Hicks and the real cycle', *The Journal of Political Economy* 60, February: 1–12.

Caldwell B, (1982) *Beyond Positivism: Economic Methodology in the Twentieth Century*, London: Allen & Unwin.

—— (ed.) (1984) *Appraisal and Criticism in Economics: A Book of Readings*, London: Allen & Unwin.

Campbell, N.R. (1920) *Foundations of Science* (formerly titled *Physics: The Elements*), republication of 1st edn 1957, New York: Dover Publications.

Campbell, T. (1981) *Seven Theories of Human Society*, Oxford: Clarendon Press.

Carlyle, T. (1883) 'On history', in G.H. Putnam (ed.) *Prose Masterpieces from Modern Essayists*, 3 vols, New York: G.P. Putnam's Sons.

Carnap, R. (1936) 'Testability and meaning', *Philosophy of Science* 3: 420–71.

—— (1937) 'Testability and meaning', *Philosophy of Science* 4: 1–40.

—— (1939) *Foundations of Logic and Mathematics*, Chicago: University of Chicago Press.

—— (1950a) 'Empiricism, semantics, and ontology', *Revue Internationale de Philosophie* 11: 20–40.

—— (1950b) *Logical Foundations of Probability*, 2nd edn 1962, Chicago: University of Chicago Press.

—— (1956) 'The methodological character of theoretical concepts', in H. Feigl and M. Scriven (eds) *The Foundations of Science and the Concepts of Psychology and Psychoanalysis*, vol. 1 of *Minnesota Studies in the Philosophy of Science*, Minneapolis: University of Minnesota Press.

Carr, D. (1961) *What is History*, ? New York: Vintage Books.

Carr, D., Dray, W., Geraets, T.F., Ouellet, F. and Watelet, H. (eds) (1982) *Philosophy of History and Contemporary Historiography*, Ottawa: University of Ottawa Press.

Cartwright, N. (1983) *How the Laws of Physics Lie*, Oxford: Oxford University Press.

—— (1989) *Nature's Capacities and their Measurement*, Oxford: Clarendon Press.

Chabod, F. (1951) *Storia della Politica estera Italiana dal 1870 al 1896*, B. Laterza (ed.), 2nd edn 1962, Bari: Editori Laterza.

Chandler, W.J. (1984) *The Science of History: A Cybernetic Approach*, New York: Gordon & Breach Science Publishers.

Cicourel, A.V. (1964) *Method and Measurement in Sociology*, Chicago: The Free Press.

Clark, G.H. (1971) *Historiography, Secular and Religious*, Nutley, N.J.: The Craig Press.

Clark, J.B. (1956) *The Distribution of Wealth*, New York: Kelley & Millman.

Clarke, D.M. (1989) *Occult Powers and Hypotheses: Cartesian Natural Philosophy under Louis XIV*, Oxford: Clarendon Press.

Coddington, A. (1972) 'Positive economics', *Canadian Journal of Economics* 5: 1–15.

Cohen, M.R. (1942) 'Causation and its application to history', *Journal of the History of Ideas* 3: 12–29.

Collingwood, R.G. (1946) *The Idea of History*, 5th edn 1962, Oxford: Oxford University Press.

Colodny, R.G. (ed.) (1962) *Frontiers of Science and Philosophy*, Pittsburgh: University of Pittsburgh.

Comte, A. (1830–42) *Cours de Philosophie Positive*, 6 vols, E. Littre (ed.), 4th edn 1877, Paris: Bachelier.

Conway, R.K., Swamy, P.A.V.B., Yanagiga, J.F., Muehlen, P. von zur (1984) 'The impossibility of causality testing', *Agricultural Economics Research* 36, 3: 1–15.

Copleston, F.C. (1961) *Aquinas*, Harmondsworth, Middlesex: Penguin Books.

Cournot, A. (1838) *Researches into the Mathematical Principles of the Theory of Wealth*, 1963 reprint, New York: Augustus M. Kelley.

Craig, W. (1956) 'Replacement of auxiliary expressions', *Philosophical Review* 65: 38–55.

Crowley, T. (ed.) (1988) *Clio's Craft: A Primer of Historical Methods*, Toronto: Copp Clark Pittman Ltd.

Davidson, D. (1984) *Essays on Actions and Events*, Oxford: Oxford University Press.

Davis, L.E. and Engerman, S. (1987) 'Cliometrics: the state of the science (or Is it art or, perhaps, witchcraft?)', *Historical Methods* 20, 3: 97–106.

Danto, A.C. (1965) *Analytical Philosophy of History*, Cambridge: Cambridge University Press.

Danto, A.C. and Morgenbesser, S. (eds) (1960) *Philosophy of Science*, New York: Meridian Books.

Doise, W. (1986) *Levels of Explanation in Social Psychology*, trans. E. Mapstone, Cambridge: Cambridge University Press.

Dolan, E.G. (ed.) (1976) *The Foundations of Modern Austrian Economics*, Kansas City: Sheed, Andrews and McNeel.

Donagan, A. (1959) 'Explanation in history', in P. Gardiner (ed.) *Theories of History*, Glencoe, Ill.: The Free Press.

—— (1974) 'Popper's examination of historicism', in E. Schilpp (ed.) *The Philosophy of Karl Popper*, La Salle, Ill.: The Open Court Press.

Doyal, L. and Harris, R. (1986) *Empiricism, Explanation and Rationality*, London: Routledge & Kegan Paul.

Dray, W.H. (1957) *Laws and Explanation in History*, 1985 edn, London: Oxford University Press.

—— (1987) *Perspectives sur l'histoire*, Ottawa: Les Presses de l'Université d'Ottawa.

Duhem, P. (1953) *The Aim and Structure of Physical Theory*, parts 1 and 2, trans. P.P. Wiener, Princeton: Princeton University Press.

Durbin, J. (1988) 'Is a philosophical consensus for statistics attainable?', *Journal of Econometrics* 37: 51–61.

Durkheim, E. (1988) *The Rules of Sociological Method*, Chicago: University of Chicago Press.

Earl, P.E. (ed.) (1988) *Psychological Economics*, Boston: Kluwer Academic Publishers.

Eberle, R., Kaplan, D. and Montague, R. (1961) 'Hempel and Oppenheim on explanation', *Philosophy of Science* 28: 418–28.

Edgeworth, F.Y. (ed.) (1925) *Papers Relating to Political Economy*, vols 1 and 3, London: The Macmillan Press Ltd.

Elster, J. (1989) 'Social norms and economic theory', *Journal of Economic Perspectives* 3, 4: 99–117.

Elton, G.R. (1967) *The Practice of History*, London: Methuen.

—— (1970) *Political History; Principles and Practice*, New York: Basic Books.

Etzioni, A. (1968) *The Active Society*, New York: The Free Press.

Evans, M.K. (1969) *Macroeconomic Activity*, New York: Harper & Row.

Febvre, L.P.V. (1953) *Combats pour l'Histoire*, 1965 edn, Paris: A. Colin.

Feigl, H. and Brodbeck, M. (eds) (1953) *Readings in the Philosophy of Science*, New York: Appleton-Century-Crofts.

Feigl, H. and Maxwell, G. (eds) (1961) *Current Issues in the Philosophy of Science*, New York: Holt, Rinehart & Winston.

Feigl, H. and Maxwell, G. (eds) (1962) *Scientific Explanation, Space, and Time*, vol. 3 of *Minnesota Studies in the Philosophy of Science*, Minneapolis: University of Minnesota Press.

Feigl, H. and Scriven, M. (eds) (1956) *The Foundations of Science and the Concepts of Psychology and Psychoanalysis*, vol. 1 of *Minnesota Studies in the Philosophy of Science*, Minneapolis: University of Minnesota Press.

Feigl, H. and Sellars, W. (eds) (1949) *Readings in Philosophical Analysis*, New York: Appleton-Century-Crofts.

Feigl, H., Scriven, M. and Maxwell, G. (eds) (1958) *Concepts, Theories, and the Mind–Body Problem*, vol. 2 of *Minnesota Studies in the Philosophy of Science*, Minneapolis: University of Minnesota Press.

Fellner, W. (1960) *Emergence and Content of Modern Economic Analysis*, New York: McGraw-Hill Book Company, Inc.

Feyerabend, P.K. (1958) 'An attempt at a realistic interpretation of experience', *Proceedings of the Aristotelian Society* 58: 143–70.

—— (1962) 'Explanation reduction and empiricism', in H. Feigl and G. Maxwell (eds) *Scientific Explanation, Space, and Time*, vol. 3 of *Minnesota*

Studies in the Philosophy of Science, Minneapolis: University of Minnesota Press.

Flamant, M. and Singer-Kérel, J. (1968) *Les Crises Economiques*, Paris: Presses Universitaires de France.

Fogel, R.W. (1982) 'Circumstantial evidence in "scientific" and traditional history', in D. Carr *et al.* (eds) *Philosophy of History and Contemporary Historiography*, Ottawa: University of Ottawa Press.

—— (1983) 'Scientific history and traditional history', in R.W. Fogel and G.R. Elton (eds) *Which Road to the Past?*, New Haven: Yale University Press.

Fogel, R.W. and Elton, G.R. (eds) (1983) *Which Road to the Past?*, New Haven: Yale University Press.

Fraassen, Bas C. van (1980) *The Scientific Image*, Oxford: Clarendon Press.

Friedman, J.W. (1986) *Game Theory with Applications to Economics*, New York: Oxford University Press.

Friedman, M. (1953) 'The methodology of positive economics', in *Essays in Positive Economics*, Chicago: University of Chicago Press.

Frisch, R.A.K. (1933) 'Propagation problems and impulse problems in dynamic economies', in *Economic Essays in Honour of Gustav Cassel*, London: Allen & Unwin Ltd, reprinted in R.A. Gordon and L.R. Klein (eds) (1965) *Readings in Business Cycles*, Homewood, Ill.: R.D. Irwin.

Fustel de Coulanges, N.D. (1891) *Histoire des Institutions Politiques de l'Ancienne France*, 6 vols, C. Jullian (ed.), 2nd edn 1901, Paris.

Gademacher, H.-G. (1989) *Truth and Method*, 2nd rev. edn, New York: Continuum.

Galileo, G. (1974) *Two New Sciences*, trans. S. Drake, Madison: University of Wisconsin Press.

Gay, P. and Cavanaugh, G.J. (eds) (1972) *Historians at Work*, vol. 1, New York: Harper & Row.

Gay, P. and Wexler, V.G. (eds) (1972) *Historians at Work*, vols 2, 3, 4, New York: Harper & Row.

Gellner, E. (1956) 'Explanation in history', *Proceedings of the Aristotelian Society*, suppl. vol. 30: 157–76.

Geweke, J. (1982) 'Causality, exogeneity, and inference' in W. Hildenbrand (ed.) *Advances in Econometrics*, Cambridge: Cambridge University Press.

—— (1973) *Cause and Meaning in the Social Sciences*, London: Routledge & Kegan Paul.

Gibbon, E. (1909–14) *Decline and Fall of the Roman Empire*, 7 vols, J.B. Bury (ed.), London: Methuen & Company.

Giddens, A. (ed.) (1974) *Positivism and Sociology*, London: Heinemann.

Giere, R.N. (1988) *Explaining Science: A Cognitive Approach*, Chicago: University of Chicago Press.

Glymour, C., Scheines, R., Spirtes, P. and Kelly, K. (eds) (1987) *Discovering Causal Structure*, Orlando, Fla.: Academic Press, Inc.

Good, I.J. (1960) 'The paradoxes of confirmation', part 1, *The British Journal for the Philosophy of Science* 11: 145–8.

—— (1961) 'The paradoxes of confirmation', part 2, *The British Journal for the Philosophy of Science* 12: 63–4.

Goode, T.M. (1977) 'Explanation, expansion, and the aims of historians:

towards an alternative account of historical explanation', *Philosophy of the Social Sciences* 7: 367–84.

Goodman, N. (1955) *Fact, Fiction, and Forecast*, Cambridge, Mass.: Cambridge University Press.

Goodwin, R.M. (1967) 'A growth cycle', in C.H. Feinstein (ed.) *Socialism Capitalism and Economic Growth: Essays Presented to M. Dobb*, London: Cambridge University Press.

Granger, C.W.J. (1969) 'Investigating causal relations by econometric models and cross-spectral methods', *Econometrica* 37: 424–38.

—— (1980) 'Generating mechanisms, models and causality', in W. Hildenbrand (ed.) *Advances in Econometrics*, Cambridge: Cambridge University Press.

Grunbaum, A. (1984) *The Foundations of Psychoanalysis*, Berkeley: University of California.

Guitton, H. (1967) *Fluctuations et Croissance Economiques*, Paris: Dalloz.

Haberler, G. (1937) *Prosperity and Depression*, 4th edn 1958, New York: Atheneum.

Habermas, J. (1971) *Knowledge and Human Interests*, trans. J.J. Shapiro, Boston: Beacon Press.

Hacking, I. (1983) *Representing and Intervening*, Cambridge: Cambridge University Press.

Hahn, F. (1982a) *Money and Inflation*, Oxford: Basil Blackwell.

—— (1982b) 'The neo-Ricardians' *Cambridge Journal of Economics* 6: 353–74.

Hahn, F. and Hollis, M. (eds) (1979) *Philosophy and Economic Theory*, Oxford: Oxford University Press.

Halévy, E. (1923) *England in 1815*, trans. E.I. Watkin and D.A. Barker, Tonbridge, Kent: Ernest Benn Ltd.

Hamouda, O.F. (1988) 'Hypothèses et réalisme', *Philosophy of Social Sciences* 18, 4: 519–21.

Hamouda, O.F. and Rowley, R. (1988a) 'Progress and production', mimeo, McGill and York Universities.

Hamouda, O.F. and Rowley, R. (1988b) *Expectations, Equilibrium and Dynamics*, New York: St. Martin's Press, Inc.

Handlin, O. (1979) *Truth in History*, Cambridge, Mass.: Harvard University Press.

Hanson, N.R. (1958) *Patterns of Discovery*, Cambridge: Cambridge University Press.

Harré, R. (1965) 'On the structure of existential judgments', *Philosophical Quarterly* 15: 43–52.

Harrod, Sir R.F. (1936) *The Trade Cycle: An Essay*, Oxford: Clarendon Press.

Hausman, D. (ed.) (1984) *The Philosophy of Economics: An Anthology*, Cambridge: Cambridge University Press.

Hawtrey, R.G. (1928) *Trade and Credit*, New York: Longmans, Green & Company.

Hayek, F.A. von (1931) *Prices and Production*, 2nd edn 1935, London: Routledge & Kegan Paul.

—— (1932–33) 'A note on the development of the doctrine of forced saving', reprinted in *Profits, Interest and Investment*, London: Routledge & Kegan Paul.

—— (1949) *Individualism and Economic Order*, London: Routledge & Kegan Paul.

—— (1974) 'The pretence of knowledge', 1989 reprint, *The American Economic Review* 79, 6: 3–7.

Heilbroner, R.L. (1973) 'Economics as a "value-free" science', *Social Research* 40: 129–43.

Heller, A. (1982) *A Theory of History*, London: Routledge & Kegan Paul.

Hempel, C.G. (1942) 'The function of general laws in history', *The Journal of Philosophy* 39: 35–48.

—— (1945a) 'Studies in the logic of confirmation', part 1, *Mind* 54, January: 1–26.

—— (1945b) 'Studies in the logic of confirmation', part 2, *Mind* 54, April: 97–121.

—— (1950) 'Problems and changes in the empiricist criterion of meaning', *Revue Internationale de Philosophie* 11: 41–65.

—— (1958) 'The theoretician's dilemma', in H. Feigl, M. Scriven and G. Maxwell (eds) *Concepts, Theories, and the Mind-Body Problem*, vol. 2 of *Minnesota Studies in the Philosophy of Science*, Minneapolis: University of Minnesota Press.

—— (1959) 'The function of general laws in history', in P. Gardiner (ed.) *Theories of History*, Glencoe, Ill.: The Free Press.

—— (1965) 'Aspects of scientific explanation', in *Aspects of Scientific Explanation and Other Essays*, New York: The Free Press.

Hempel, C.G. and Oppenheim, P. (1948) 'Studies in the logic of explanation', *Philosophy of Science* 15: 135–75.

Hendry, D.F. (1985) 'Econometric methodology: a personal perspective', in T.F. Bewley (ed.) *Advances in Econometrics*, vol. 2, Cambridge: Cambridge University Press.

Hertz, H.R. (1956) *The Principles of Mechanics, Presented in a New Form*, trans. D.E. Jones and J.T. Walley, New York: Dover Publications.

Hesse, M. (1958) 'Theories, dictionaries and observation', *British Journal for the Philosophy of Science* 9: 12–28, 128–9.

—— (1962) 'On what there is in physics', *British Journal for the Philosophy of Science* 13: 234–44.

Hicks, J.R. (1939) *Value and Capital*, 2nd edn 1946, Oxford: Oxford University Press.

—— (1950) *A Contribution to the Theory of the Trade Cycle*, Oxford: Oxford University Press.

—— (1976) '"Revolution" in economics' in S. Latsis (ed.) *Method and Appraisal in Economics*, Cambridge: Cambridge University Press.

—— (1979) *Causality in Economics*, New York: Basic Books Inc.

—— (1984) 'Is economics a science?', *Interdisciplinary Science Reviews* 9, 3: 213–18.

Holland, P.W. (1986) 'Statistics and causal inference', *Journal of the American Statistical Association* 81: 945–60; see also comment by C. Glymour 'Statistics and metaphysics', Ibid: 964–6, and by C. Granger 'Comment', Ibid: 967–8, followed by P.W. Holland 'Rejoinder', Ibid: 968–70.

Hildenbrand, W. (1982) *Advances in Econometrics*, Cambridge: Cambridge University Press.

Hollis, M. (1977) *Models of Man*, Cambridge: Cambridge University Press.

Hood, W.C. and Koopmans, T.C. (eds) (1953) *Studies in Econometric Method*, New York: John Wiley & Sons, Inc.

Hosiasson-Lindenbaum, J. (1940) 'On confirmation', *The Journal of Symbolic Logic* 5: 133–48.

Hospers, J. (1946) 'On explanation', *Journal of Philosophy* 4: 337–56.

Hume, D. (1790) *History of England*, 8 vols, 1822 edn, London: Richard Priestly.

—— (1739–40) *Treatise on Human Nature*, T.H. Green and T.H. Grose (eds), new edn 1878, London: Longmans.

Hutchison, T.W. (1938) *The Significance and Basic Postulates of Economic Theory*, 1960 reprint, New York: Augustus M. Kelley.

—— (1977) *Knowledge and Ignorance in Economics*, Chicago: University of Chicago Press.

—— (1978) *On Revolutions and Progress in Economic Knowledge*, Cambridge: Cambridge University Press.

Iggers, G.G. and Parker, H.T. (eds) (1979) *International Handbook of Historical Studies*, Westport, Conn.: Greenwood Press.

Irvine, J., Miles, I. and Evans, J. (eds) (1979) *Demystifying Social Statistics*, London: Pluto Press.

Jevons, W.S. (1871) *The Theory of Political Economy*, 4th edn 1911, London: The Macmillan Press Ltd.

Johnston, J. (1963) *Econometric Methods*, 2nd edn 1972, Tokyo: McGraw-Hill Kogakusha, Ltd.

Judge, G.G., Griffiths, W.E., Hill, R.C., Lutkepohl, H. and Lee, T.C. (eds) (1980) *The Theory and Practice of Econometrics*, 2nd edn 1985, New York: John Wiley & Sons.

Kadish, A. (1989) *Historians, Economists and Economic History*, London: Routledge.

Kahl, R. (ed.) (1963) *Studies in Explanation: A Reader in the Philosophy of Science*, Englewood Cliffs, N.J.: Prentice-Hall, Inc.

Kalecki, M. (1936) 'A theory of the business cycle', *Review of Economic Studies* 4, 2: 77–97.

Kant, I. (1933) *Critique of Pure Reason*, trans. N.K. Smith, London: The Macmillan Press Ltd.

Kaplan, D. (1961) 'Explanation revisited', *Philosophy of Science* 28: 429–36.

Katona, G. (1951) *Psychological Analysis of Economic Behaviour*, New York: McGraw-Hill.

—— (1975) *Psychological Economics*, New York: Elsevier.

—— (1979) 'Toward a macropsychology', *American Psychologist* 34: 118–26.

—— (1980) *Essays on Behavioural Economics*, Ann Arbour, Mich.: University of Michigan, Institute for Social Research.

Katzner, D.W. (1983) *Analysis Without Measurement*, Cambridge: Cambridge University Press.

Keynes, J.M. (1921) *A Treatise On Probability*, vol. 8 of *The Collected Writings of John Maynard Keynes*, 1973, D. Moggridge (ed.), New York: St. Martin's Press.

—— (1933) *Essays in Biography*, London: The Macmillan Press Ltd.

—— (1936) *The General Theory of Employment, Interest and Money*, London: The Macmillan Press Ltd.

—— (1973b) *The General Theory and After*, vol. 14 of The Collected Writings of John Maynard Keynes, D. Moggridge (ed.), New York: St. Martin's Press.

Keynes, J.N. (1891) *The Scope and Method of Political Economy*, 1963 reprint of 4th edn 1917, New York: Augustus M. Kelley.

Klamer, A., McCloskey, D.N. and Solow, R.M. (eds) (1988) *The Consequences of Economic Rhetoric*, Cambridge: Cambridge University Press.

Klein, L.R. (ed.) (1954) *Contributions of Survey Methods to Economics*, New York: Columbia University Press.

—— (1988) 'The statistical approach to economics', *Journal of Econometrics* 37: 7–26.

Koopmans, T.C. (ed.) (1950) *Statistical Inference in Dynamic Economic Models*, New York: John Wiley & Sons, Inc.

—— (1957) *Three Essays on the State of Economic Science*, New York: McGraw-Hill.

Kuhn, T.S. (1962) *The Structure of Scientific Revolutions*, 2nd edn 1970, Chicago: University of Chicago Press.

Kyburg, H.E. (1964) 'Recent work in inductive logic', *American Philosophical Quarterly* 1: 249–87.

Kydland, F.E. and Prescott, E.C. (1982) 'Time to build and aggregate fluctuations', *Econometrica* 50: 1345–70.

Laidler, D. (1977) *The Demand for Money*, New York: Dun-Donnelley.

Langlois, C.V. and Seignobos, C. (1898) *An Introduction to the Study of History*, trans. G. Berry, New York: Holt, Rinehart & Winston.

Laudan, L. (1984) *Science and Values*, Berkeley: University of California Press.

Lawson, H. and Appignanesi, L. (eds) (1989) *Dismantling Truth*, London: Weidenfeld & Nicolson.

Lawson, T. (1987) 'The relative absolute nature of knowledge and economic analysis', *The Economic Journal* 97: 951–70.

—— (1989a) 'Abstraction, tendencies and stylised facts: a realist approach to economic analysis', *Cambridge Journal of Economics* 13: 59–78.

—— (1989b) 'Realism and instrumentalism in the development of econometrics', *Oxford Economic Papers* 41: 236–58.

Leamer, E.E. (1983) 'Let's take the con out of econometrics', *The American Economic Review* 73, 1: 31–43.

Lear, J. (1988) *Aristotle: The Desire to Understand*, Cambridge: Cambridge University Press.

Lefebvre, G. (1963) *Études sur la révolution Française*, 2nd rev. edn, Paris: Presses Universitaires de France.

Leijonhufvnd, A. (1985) 'Ideology and analysis in macroecnomics', in P. Koslowsky (ed.), *Economics and Philosophy*, Tubingen: J.C.B. Mohr.

Lerner, D. (ed.) (1965) *Causes and Effects*, New York: The Free Press.

Lewis, C.I. (1946) *An Analysis of Knowledge and Valuation*, 1962 edn, La Salle, Ill.: The Open Court Publishing Company.

Lewis, C.S. (1964) *The Discarded Image*, Cambridge: Cambridge University Press.

Linsky, L. (ed.) (1952) *Semantics and the Philosophy of Language*, Urbana, Ill.: University of Illinois Press.

Lipsey, R. (1963) *An Introduction to Positive Economics*, 1st ed., London: Weidenfeld and Nicholson.

Lucas, R.E. Jr (1981) *Studies in Business-Cycle Theory*, Oxford: Basil Blackwell.

—— (1987) *Models of Business Cycles*, Oxford: Basil Blackwell.

Lundberg, E.F. (1937) *Studies in the Theory of Economic Expansion*, 1964 reprint, New York: Augustus M. Kelley.

Lyndhurst, C. (1976) *The Use of Models in the Social Sciences*, Boulder: Westview Press, Inc.

Mabillon, J. (1789) *De Re Diplomatica*, 2 vols, J. Adimari (ed.), 3rd edn, Naples: Luteciae-Parisiorum.

McCloskey, D.N. (1983) 'The rhetoric of economics', *Journal of Economic Literature* 21: 481–517.

—— (1990 'Ancients and Moderns', *Social Science History* 14, 3: 289–303.

Machlup, F. (1955) 'The problem of verification in economics', *Southern Economic Journal* 22, 1: 1–21.

—— (1961) 'Are the social sciences really inferior?', in W.L. Marr and B. Raj (eds) *How Economists Explain*, Lanham, Md: University Press of America.

—— (1978) *Methodology of Economics and Other Social Sciences*, New York: Academic Press.

McKenzie, R.B. and Tullock, G. (1975) *The New World of Economics*, 3rd edn 1981, Homewood, Ill.: Richard D. Irwin, Inc.

Mackie, J.L. (1980) *The Cement of the Universe: A Study of Causation*, Oxford: Oxford University Press.

Malinvaud, E. (1978) *The Theory of Unemployment Reconsidered*, Oxford: Basil Blackwell.

Malthus, T.R. (1827) *Definitions in Political Economy*, 1963 reprint of original edn, New York: Augustus M. Kelley.

Mandelbaum, M. (1938) *The Problem of Historical Knowledge*, New York: Liveright Publishing Corporation.

—— (1942) 'Causation in historical events', *Journal of the History of Ideas* 3: 30–50.

Margolis, J. (1987) *Science Without Unity*, Oxford: Basil Blackwell.

Marr, W.L. and Raj, B. (eds) (1983) *How Economists Explain*, Lanham, Md: University Press of America.

Marschak, J. (1950) 'Statistical inference in economics: an introduction', in T.C. Koopmans (ed.) *Statistical Inference in Dynamic Economic Models*, New York: John Wiley & Sons.

Marshall, A. (1890) *Principles of Economics*, 8th edn 1920, London: The Macmillan Press Ltd.

Marx, K. (1857–8) 'Ideology and method in political economy', in *Grundisse: Foundations of the Critique of Political Economy*, (1973) trans. M. Nicolaus, reprinted in D.M. Hausman (ed.) *The Philosophy of Economics: An Anthology*, Cambridge: Cambridge University Press.

—— (1976) *Le Capital*, trans. J. Roy, Montréal: Nouvelle Frontière.

Matthen, M. (ed.) (1987) *Aristotle Today*, Edmonton: Academic Printing & Publishing.

Maxwell, G. (1961) 'Meaning postulates in scientific theories', in H. Feigl and G. Maxwell (ed.) *Current Issues in the Philosophy of Science*, New York: Holt, Rinehart & Winston.

—— (1962) 'The ontological status of theoretical entities', in H. Feigl and G. Maxwell (eds) *Scientific Explanations, Space, and Time*, vol. 3 of *Minnesota Studies in the Philosophy of Science*, Minneapolis: University of Minnesota Press.

Mayer, T. (1980) 'Economics as a hard science: realistic goal or wishful thinking?', *Economic Inquiry* 18: 165–78.

Miles, I. (1985) *Social Indicators for Human Development*, London: Frances Pinter.

Mill, J.S. (1843) *System of Logic*, 8th edn 1872, London: Longmans, Green, Reader & Dyer.

—— (1950) *Philosophy of Scientific Method*, ed. E. Nagel, New York: Hafner Publishing Company.

Mirowski, P. (1988) *Against Mechanism: Protecting Economics from Science*, Totowa, NJ: Rowman and Littlefield.

—— (1989) 'The measurement without theory controversy', *Economies et Sociétés*, Série Oeconomia-PE 11: 65–87.

Mises, L.E. von (1933) *Epistemological Problems of Economics*, trans. G. Reisman, 2nd edn 1960, Princeton, N.J.: Van Nostrand.

—— (1945) *Human Action: A Treatise on Economics*, London: William Hodge.

Mitchell, W.C. (1923) 'Business cycles', in *Business Cycles and Unemployment*, New York: McGraw-Hill.

Mongin, P. (1988) 'Le réalisme des hypothèses et la partial interprétation view', *Philosophy of the Social Sciences* 18, 3: 281–325.

Morrison, M. (1989) 'Theory, intervention and realism', *Synthèse* 82, 1: 1–22.

Mulkay, M. (1980) *Science and the Sociology of Knowledge*, London: Allen & Unwin.

Murphey, M.G. (1973) *Our Knowledge of the Historical Past*, Indianapolis: Bobbs-Merrill.

Nagel, E. (1950) *John Stuart Mill's Philosophy of Scientific Method*, New York: Hafner Publishing Company.

—— (1952) 'Some issues in the logic of historical analysis', *Scientific Monthly* 74, March: 162–9.

—— (1961) *The Structure of Science*, New York: Harcourt, Brace & World.

—— (1963) 'Assumptions in Economic Theory', *American Economic Review. Papers and Proceedings*, May: 211–19.

Nagel, E., Suppes, P. and Tarski, A. (eds) (1962) *Logic, Methodology and Philosophy of Science*, Stanford: Stanford University Press.

Natanson, M. (ed.) (1970) *Phenomenology and Social Reality*, The Hague: Martinus Nijhoff.

Nicod, J. (1950) *Foundations of Geometry and Induction*, trans. P. P. Weiner, London: Routledge & Kegan Paul.

Nowell-Smith, P.H. (1970) 'Historical explanation', in *Mind, Science, and History, Contemporary Philosophic Thought*, International Philosophy Year Conferences at Brockport, vol. 2, Albany, N.Y.: New York State University Press.

—— (1981) 'History as patterns of thought and action', in *Substance and Form in History*, Edinburgh: Edinburgh University Press.

Oldroyd, D. (1986) *The Arch of Knowledge*, New York: Methuen.

Oser, J. (1963) *The Evolution of Economic Thought*, New York: Harcourt, Brace and World, Inc.

Pap, A. (1962) *An Introduction to the Philosophy of Science*, New York: Free Press of Glencoe.

Pears, D.F. (1950) 'Hypotheticals', *Analysis* 10: 49–63.

Pheby, J. (1988) *Methodology and Economics*, London: Macmillan.

Pieters, R.G.M. (1988) 'Attitude-behaviour relationships', in W.F. van Raaij, G.M. van Veldhoven and K.E. Warneryd (eds) *Handbook of Economic Psychology*, Dordrecht: Kluwer Academic Press.

Pigou, A.C. (ed.) (1925) *Memorials of Alfred Marshall*, London: Macmillan and Co. Ltd.

Pirenne, H. (1931) 'What are historians trying to do?', in S.A. Rice (ed.) *Methods in Social Sciences*, Chicago: Chicago University Press.

Plott, C.R. and Smith, V.L. (1978) 'An experimental examination of two exchange institutions', *Review of Economic Studies* 45: 133–53.

Popper, Sir K.R. (1936) Lecture on 'The poverty of historicism', Brussels; later published in *The Open Society and its Enemies* (1945), London: Routledge & Kegan Paul, and *The Poverty of Historicism* (1957, 1961), Routledge & Kegan Paul.

—— (1950) *The Logic of Scientific Discovery*, 2nd edn 1959, Toronto: University of Toronto Press.

—— (1957) 'The aim of science', *Ratio* 1: 24–35.

—— (1963) 'Three views concerning human knowledge', in *Conjectures and Refutations: The Growth of Scientific Knowledge*, New York: Basic Books Inc.

Pratt, J.W. and Schlaifer, R. (1988) 'On the interpretation and observation of laws', *Journal of Econometrics* 39: 23–52.

Price, H.H. (1953) *Thinking and Experience*, Cambridge: Harvard University Press.

Putnam, H. (1962a) 'The analytic and the synthetic', in H. Feigl and G. Maxwell (eds) *Scientific Explanation, Space, and Time*, vol. 3 of *Minnesota Studies in the Philosophy of Science*, Minneapolis: University of Minnesota Press.

—— (1962b) 'What theories are not', in E. Nagel *et al.* (eds) *Logic, Methodology and Philosophy of Science*, Stanford: Stanford University Press.

—— (1981) *Reason, Truth and History*, Cambridge: Cambridge University Press.

Quesnay, F. (1972) *Tableau Economique*, trans. M. Kuczynski and R. L. Meek (eds), London: The Macmillan Press Ltd; New York: Augustus M. Kelley.

Quine, W.V.O. (1948) 'On what there is', *Review of Metaphysics* 2: 21–38.

—— (1951) 'Two dogmas of empiricism', *Philosophical Review* 60: 20–43.

Raaij, W.F. van, Veldhoven, G.M. van and Warneryd, K.E. (eds) (1988) *Handbook of Economic Psychology*, Dordrecht: Kluwer Academic Publishers.

Raffel, S. (1976) *Matters of Fact*, London: Routledge & Kegan Paul.

Ramsey, F.P. (1931) 'Theories', in *The Foundation of Mathematics and Other Logical Essays*, London: Routledge & Kegan Paul.

Ranke, L. von (1973) *The Theory and Practice of History*, G.G. Iggers and K. von Moltke (eds), trans. W.A. Iggers and K. von Moltke, Indianapolis: Bobbs-Merrill Company Inc.

—— (1976) *Histories of the Latin and Teutonic Nations 1494–1514*, rev. trans. G.R. Dennis, New York: AMS Press.

Reese, W.L. (ed.) (1963) *Philosophy of Science: The Delaware Seminar*, vol. 2, New York: Interscience Publishers.

Robertson, D.H. (1926) *Banking Policy and the Price Level*, 1949 reprint, New York: Augustus M. Kelley.

—— (1933) 'Saving and hoarding', *Economic Journal* 43: 399–413, reprinted in *Essays in Monetary Theory* (1940), London: King.

Rosenberg, A. (1988) 'The past recaptured: Mongin on the problem of realism in economics', *Philosophy of the Social Sciences* 18, 3: 379–81.

Rozeboom, W.W. (1962) 'The factual content of theoretical concepts', in H. Feigl and G. Maxwell (eds) *Scientific Explanation, Space, and Time*, vol. 3 of *Minnesota Studies in the Philosophy of Science*, Minneapolis: University of Minnesota Press.

Russell, B. (1940) *An Inquiry into Meaning and Truth*, London: Allen & Unwin Ltd.

—— (1948) *Human Knowledge*, London: Allen & Unwin Ltd.

Samuelson, P.A. (1965) 'Some notes on causality and teleology in economics', in D. Lerner (ed.) *Cause and Effect*, New York: The Free Press.

Sassower, R. (1985) *Philosophy of Economics*, Boston: University Press of America.

Say, J.B. (1880) *A Treatise on Political Economy*, 1971 reprint, New York: Augustus M. Kelley.

Schabus, M. (1986) 'An Assessment of the Scientific Standing of Economics', *Philosophy of Science Association 1986* 1: 298–306.

Scheffler, I. (1957) 'Prospects of a modest empiricism', *Review of Metaphysics* 10: 1–42.

—— (1963) *The Anatomy of Inquiry*, New York: Knopf.

Schumpeter, J.A. (1954) *History of Economic Analysis*, New York: Oxford University Press.

Sellars, W. (1961) 'The language of theories', in H. Feigl and G. Maxwell (eds) *Current Issues in the Philosophy of Science*, New York: Holt, Rinehart & Winston.

—— (1962) 'Philosophy and the scientific image of man', in R.G. Colodny (ed.) *Frontiers of Science and Philosophy*, Pittsburgh: University of Pittsburgh.

—— (1963) 'Theoretical explanation', in W.L. Reese (ed.) *Philosophy of Science: The Delaware Seminar*, vol. 2, New York: Interscience Publishers.

Senior, N.W. (1836) *An Outline of the Science of Political Economy*, 7th edn 1938, New York: Augustus M. Kelley, Inc.

Shackle, G.L.S. (1972) *Epistemics and Economics*, Cambridge: Cambridge University Press.

—— (1979) *Imagination and the Nature of Choice*, Edinburgh: Edinburgh University Press.

Simon, H.A. (1953) 'Causal ordering and identifiability', in W. C. Hood and T.C. Koopmans (eds) *Studies in Econometric Method*, New York: John Wiley & Sons.

Skinner, B.F. (1972) *Beyond Freedom and Dignity*, New York: Bantam.

Skyrms, B. (1988) 'Probability and causation', *Journal of Econometrics* 39: 53–68.

Slutsky, E. (1937) 'The summation of random causes as the source of cyclic processes', *Econometrica* 5: 105–46.

Smart, J.J.C. (1963) *Philosophy and Scientific Realism*, New York: Humanities Press.

Smith, A. (1776) *An Inquiry into the Nature and Causes of the Wealth of Nations*, 1937 reprint, New York: The Modern Library.

Smith, V.L. (1980) 'Relevance of laboratory experiments to testing resource allocation theory', in J. Kmenta and J. Ramsey (eds) *Evaluation of Econometric Models*, New York: Academic Press.

—— (1982) 'Microeconomic systems as an experimental science', *American Economic Review* 72: 923–55.

Stone, L. (1972) *The Causes of the English Revolution: 1529–1642*, London: Routledge & Kegan Paul

—— (1977) *The Family, Sex and Marriage 1500–1800*, New York: Harper & Row.

—— (1988) *The Past and the Present Revisited*, London: Routledge & Kegan Paul.

Stone, R. (1966) *Mathematics in the Social Sciences and Other Essays*, London: Chapman and Hall Ltd.

Strawson, P.F. (1959) *Individuals: An Essay in Descriptive Metaphysics*, London: Methuen.

Sugden, R. (1989) 'Spontaneous order', *Journal of Economic Perspectives* 3, 4: 95–7.

Swamy, P.A.V.B., Conway, R.K. and Muehlen, P. von zur 'The foundations of econometrics', *Econometrics Review* 4, 1: 1–61.

Taggart, F.J. (1942) 'Causation in historical events', *Journal of the History of Ideas* 3: 3–11.

Taylor, C. (1985) *Collected Papers*, Vol. 1: *Human Agency and Language*; vol. 2; *Philosophy and the Human Sciences*, Cambridge: Cambridge University Press.

Theil, H. (1971) *Principles of Econometrics*, New York: John Wiley & Sons, Inc.

Thomas, D. (1979) *Naturalism and Social Science: A Post-Empiricist Philosophy of Social Science*, Cambridge: Cambridge University Press.

Toulmin, S. (1953) *The Philosophy of Science: An Introduction*, London: Hutchinson's University Library.

Trevelyan, G.M. (1938) *The English Revolution*, London: T. Butterworth Ltd.

—— (1949) 'Bias in history', in *An Autobiography and Other Essays*, London: Longmans, Green & Company.

Trigg, R. (1982) *The Shaping of Man: Philosophical Aspects of Sociobiology*, Oxford: Basil Blackwell.

Trueman, J.H. (1967) *The Anatomy of History*, Toronto: J.M. Dent and Sons Ltd.

Turgot, A.R.J. (1767) *Observations sur un mémoire de M. de Saint-Peravy*, republished in *Oeuvres*, D. de Nemours (ed.) (1808), Paris.

—— (1770) *Reflections on the Formation and the Distribution of Riches*, 1963 reprint, New York: Augustus M. Kelley.

Valla, L. (1922) *The Treatise of Lorenzo Valla on the Donation of Constantine*, trans. C.B. Coleman, New Haven: Yale University Press.

Vernon, M. (1966) 'Perception, Attention and Consciousness' in Paul Bahan (ed.), *Attention*, Princeton: Van Nostrand.

Veyne, P. (1971) *Writing History: Essay on Epistemology*, trans. M. Moore-Rinvolucri, Manchester: Manchester University Press.

Vives, J.L. (1969) *An Economic History of Spain*, trans. F.M. Lopez-Morillas, Princeton, N.J.: Princeton University Press.

Voltaire (1963) *Essai sur les mœurs et l'Esprit des Nations*, Paris: Editions Garnier.

Wallace, W.A. (1974) *Causality and Scientific Explanation*, vol. 2, Ann Arbor: The University of Michigan Press.

Walras, L. (1954) *Elements of Pure Economics*, London: Allen & Unwin Ltd.

Walsh, W.H. (1961) 'The limits of scientific history', in J. Hogan (ed.) *Historical Studies III*, London.

Warneryd, K.E. (1988a) 'Social influence on economic behaviour', in W.F. van Raaij *et al.* (eds) *Handbook of Economic Psychology*, Dordrecht: Kluwer Academic Press.

—— (1988b) 'Economic psychology as a field of study', in W.F. van Raaij *et al.* (eds) *Handbook of Economic Psychology*, Dordrecht: Kluwer Academic Press.

Watkins, J.W.N. (1968) 'Methodological individualism and social tendencies', in M. Brodbeck (ed.) *Readings in the Philosophy of Social Science*, New York: The Macmillan Press, Ltd.

Webb, D.A. (1944) 'The place of mathematics in scientific method', *Hermathena* 64: 64–87.

Weber, M. (1949) 'Objectivity and understanding in economics', trans. E.A. Shilz and H.A. Finch in D.M. Hausman (ed.) (1984) *The Philosophy Of Economics: An Anthology*, Cambridge: Cambridge University Press.

Wegman, E.J. (1986) 'Some personal recollection of Harold Cramer on the development of statistics and probability', *Statistical Science* 1: 528–35.

Weick, C. (1968) 'Systematic Observational Methods' in Gardner, Lindzey and Elliot Aronson (eds), the *Handbook of Social Psychology*, vol. 2, Mass.: Addison-Wesley.

White, H. (1973) *Metahistory: The Historical Imagination in Nineteenth-Century Europe*, Baltimore: The Johns Hopkins University Press.

White, M. (1965) *Foundations of Historical Knowledge*, New York: Harper & Row.

Wicksell, K. (1898) *Interest and Prices*, trans. R.F. Kahn, 1962 reprint, New York: Augustus M. Kelley.

Willer, D. and Willer, J. (1973) *Systematic Empiricism: Critique of a Pseudoscience*, Englewood Cliffs, N.J.: Prentice-Hall, Inc.

Winch, P. (1958) *The Idea of a Social Science*, London: Routledge & Kegan Paul.

Wirst, P. and Woolley, P. (1982) *Social Relations and Human Attributes*, London: Tavistock.

Wisdom, J.O. (1987) *Philosophy of the Social Sciences*, vols 1 and 2, Aldershot: Gower Publishing Company.

Wright, G.H. von (1957) *The Logical Problem of Induction*, 2nd edn, Oxford: Basil Blackwell.

Zeller, E. (1962) *Stoics, Epicureans and Sceptics*, trans. O.J. Reichel, new and rev. edn, New York: Russell & Russell.

Zellner, A. (1984) *Basic Issues in Econometrics*, Chicago: University of Chicago Press.

—— (1988) 'Causality and causal laws in economics', *Journal of Econometrics* 39: 7–21.

Index